UNIQUE EATS AND EATERIES

OF

HOUSTON

Library of Congress Control Number: 2018962452
ISBN: 9781681061986

Book Design: Barbara Northcott

Printed in the United States of America
19 20 21 22 23 5 4 3 2 1

UNIQUE EATS AND EATERIES

OF

HOUSTON

SAM BROWN

CONTENTS

ACKNOWLEDGMENTS

To my wife, the shrimp boat captain of my heart. Thanks for the notes.

To my Beau-Guy, Mila, and Abigail Josey Brown. Whooped Em Again. *Ik hou van je lullen.*

To my mom, who taught me pretty much everything.

To my dad. I miss you very much.

To my friends: thank you. You are incredible.

A Special Thank You to Amanda Medsger and Jamay Caturabi, Dave, The Sloans, The Covingtons, The Mclellans, Knox, Lucas's red knees, Charuk, Jim, Danny, Van, Chris, Kenny, Harris, Andrea, The Guerins, and The Gannons.

Thanks Robert Mullens and Joel Carter.

Thank you, Cuellars.

Love you, Zoey-dog.

My gratitude to the wonderful people I met while writing this. Thanks for your hard work.

To all my former students: See? I told you. Work hard and anything is possible.

To my former colleagues and every teacher in the world: You are amazing.

Finally, the most important thing is that I do not dedicate this book to Matt Kelly. Not one bit.

INTRODUCTION

Anyone can go online to read restaurant reviews.

I encourage it, in fact, as I don't claim to be an expert. I'm also not a critic. Critics occasionally have to write negative reviews. That's not what this book is. All the places listed are good.

Who would read a restaurant book with bad reviews in it? That's precisely what the Internet is for. Thousands of angry bloggers and Yelpers are there to fill every petty and critical need one may have. Their photos are in color and each detail of their meal is deconstructed, so anyone can read all about how a waiter brought the wrong fork and just ruined Ashleigh's 21st birthday.

That is not Houston, though. It isn't even reality.

Visitors will find something the locals already know. Respect, tradition, and kindness run deep in Space City. Hell, you don't even have to read the rest of this book to learn that. (Thanks for buying it, though.)

Go out; drink and eat. Meet new people and shoot the breeze. Buy a round of beers. Learn to play horseshoes, maybe.

Houstonians are fairly laid-back in most regards. There are definitely some topics most locals have zero qualms entering into heated debate over, though. Certain subjects like football, food, and why Dallas is a terrible city evoke great passion.

Food is the most important thing on that list.

Ask a local what they think the best Tex-Mex restaurant is, for example, and it will soon be apparent how important food is to Houstonians. People here will defend to the death their favorite brisket spot or bowl of pho. We are passionate about such things, silly as it may seem.

Most importantly, know that everyone is welcome. Always.

Houston was the first major American city to elect an openly gay mayor. (What up, Anise?)

Houston is DJ Screw and Paul Wall, baby.

Beyoncé is from here. That bears repeating. Beyoncé is from here.

Houston doesn't have walls because there are no real divisions. It's a place of warmth, shown consistently in our compassion for one another. It's also literally warm, as evidenced during the horrible, underpants-soaking humidity of the long summers.

We are NASA, Bill Hicks, Bluebonnets, Bun B, JJ Watt, James Harden, CP3, and Jose Altuve.

We also have food unlike anywhere else, and whether it's burgers or borscht, it is here somewhere.

Houston may be the fourth-largest city in America, but it is quite possibly the best place in the country to dine out, at least in terms of value and variety.

Unique eats and eateries can be found all over Houston—too many for one book, even. Each and every visitor to any of our 10,000-plus restaurants will find a staggering array of cuisines available from every imaginable culture and country.

So there's really only one thing to do.

Try it out.

UNIQUE EATS AND EATERIES

OF

HOUSTON

AXELRAD AND LUIGI'S PIZZA

At the risk of sounding disloyal to my hometown, the easiest description of the scene around Luigi's is Austin-esque. It's a bit Austin-y. Even somewhat Austin-ish.

However, this isn't a book about Austin. Austin can stay weird. I'll stay in Houston.

Luigi's has been a well-established, beloved family pizza joint serving New York–style classics in a comfortable, friendly setting since opening in 2008. There is limited seating inside, but the outdoor patio has wooden tables on a covered deck for overflow. Luigi's was—and is—a requisite destination for pizza lovers. However, the area around Luigi's wasn't exactly a be-boppin' hotspot.

That changed in 2015 when beer-centric bar Axelrad opened next door in a refurbished general store. Capable of supporting hundreds of guests, their hip outdoor beer garden and patio offers tables, chairs, benches, and hammocks for an artsy, breezy vibe. Luigi's partnership with Axelrad is a collective homage to all things pizza and beer, and it has become a popular gathering point for the diverse clientele packing both places most nights.

Independent of each other, Luigi's and Axelrad would still draw regular crowds. Operating in tandem facilitates the perfect symbiotic environment for gathering friends to eat, drink, and be merry.

Axelrad's generous selection of craft beer, mixed drinks, and wine promises that hungry bar goers will be adequately primed prior to pizza time. The bar also hosts food trucks and pop-ups from local chefs and restaurants if pizza isn't in the cards. Frozen drinks and craft beer buckets are sold at Axelrad to enjoy on their expansive outdoor seating area, a dog and family-friendly open space with picnic tables to relax around.

Left: Axelrad's courtyard reflects its status as an artsy place, with lots of murals and paintings.

Middle: Gelato pop. It's outrageously good. Ask the bartenders to unlock the freezer for one.

Right: Some slices from Luigi's: two giant, crispy triangles of pure joy.

Axelrad also boasts a full menu of rotating cocktails and an always intriguing draught beer selection.

Luigi's has always been—and continues to be—BYOB. Save a few bucks by bringing in some favorite wine or beer to enjoy alongside their excellent Caprese pizza with buffalo mozzarella and prosciutto.

If living well matters, finish up with some handcrafted gelato popsicles from inside Axelrad, particularly the glazed donut with sprinkles. The food is wonderful and simply delicious. Diners seeking the best of both worlds would be smart to order first from Luigi's. Grab a number and head on to Axelrad's spacious courtyard for a wider variety of drinks. Sip on a craft beer and chill out—a runner will deliver food hot and fresh from Luigi's ovens.

3700 Almeda Road
Houston, TX 77004
281-793-3333, luigispizzahouston.com

GOODE COMPANY BBQ

One day in 1977, a good man named Jim Goode found himself annoyed while sitting in an empty barbecue restaurant called Red Barn on Kirby.

Perhaps his annoyance was projection—maybe the lack of customers and lazy employees echoed his own internal frustrations. After all, he had been working as a freelance advertising artist, struggling with uncertainties of inconsistent work, tedious clients, and irregular payment. Whatever his reason, when the proprietor noticed his chagrin and asked why he was sour, his response was classic Jim Goode—terse, honest, and personable—and a reason why Houston enjoys the bounty of his good fortunes since that frustrating day.

After he got talking with the owner, Goode ended up asking how much she wanted for the place. She originally started the business with her husband, who had recently passed away. The business was failing, and her heart just wasn't in it.

This was an opportunity, he reckoned. Goode decided to remedy his dissatisfaction with corporate work and start his own restaurant. It was the beginning of a restaurant empire that has dominated Houston's dining scene since.

Utilizing a pioneering, slow-smoking technique with mesquite wood, Jim and his Uncle Joe Dixie developed Goode Company Barbeque, shifting the fortunes of his family forever. They practically lived at the restaurant the first year according to Jim's son, rotating inside and outside during nightly vigils, taking turns guarding their slow-smoked meat with shotguns.

Their commitment paid off, and there are now three Goode Company Barbeque locations serving Jim's perfectly smoked barbecued meats, as well as two locations for Goode Company Seafood, two GC Kitchen & Cantinas and GC Hamburgers &

Top Left: Honesty on a sign equates to honesty on a plate.

Top Middle: Lines wrap around the corner during the holidays for the famous pecan pie.

Top Right: Smoked turkey on jalapeño cheddar bread, doused in sauce.

Bottom Left: One lonely rib, ostracized by its rib brethren.

Bottom Right: Austin baked beans are worthy of a visit on their own.

Taqueria. Goode Company most recently opened Goode's Armadillo Palace in 2017, a tribute to all things Texas serving a hodgepodge of the other menus in a pleasantly boisterous honky-tonk setting.

Goode Company Barbeque remains the standard, and visitors would be hard-pressed to not enjoy the fresh-baked, thick-cut jalapeño cheddar bread. The house sauce is a perfect accompaniment of spicy, tomato-based perfection. There is beer on ice and dirty rice with echoes of Cajun influence, along with regional sweets like pecan pie and chilled chocolate cream pie to combat the Houston heat.

Goode's Austin baked beans are sweet, spicy, and smoky, featuring apples simmered with bits of meat and pinto beans. It's one of my all-time favorite dishes. Seriously, order a couple sides of it. They are so damn good.

5109 Kirby Avenue
Houston, TX 77098
713-522-2530, goodecompany.com

THE MAPLE LEAF

Ice hockey is a sickness. The only cure is more ice hockey.

Football is violent, but hockey is violence. TV doesn't do justice to how fast and truly brutal hockey can be.

So, word of advice: don't ask for a channel change at The Maple Leaf when hockey is on. Canadian through and through, a local game might play on a side TV, but The Maple Leaf is a hockey pub before all else.

Naturally, The Maple Leaf serves poutine, only in a number of creative and fun variations. There's also an option for tater tots rather than the more traditional French fries. The pub's Texican poutine is a facelift for the famous food of Canada, but with local flavors like queso, cotija cheese, pico de gallo, and guacamole.

For beer, there's Molson and Labatt Blue. There's also plenty of great specials, like a steak night and $12 pitchers of domestic beers every Thursday. Plenty of good burgers, wings, and standard pub fare keep stomachs full while darts, pool, mini hockey, and poker tournaments keep idle hands occupied.

The massive surrounding apartment complexes in Midtown Houston makes it easy to overlook The Maple Leaf. It's has a neighborhood vibe, though. Sean and Olivia Blair own and operate the pub, taking great pride in creating an environment that welcomes one and all. Relaxed, pleasant, and utterly unpretentious—both in spirit and practice—makes the Leaf a perfect spot to eat and drink.

Loving ice hockey helps, too, but is not required.

514 Elgin Street
Houston, TX 77006
713-520-6464, themapleleafpub.com

Left: Drink in an old penalty box. Drink too much and get put into a real-life penalty box: jail.

Top Right: It's an extra two points if you can throw the dart dead center into the leaf. You'll have some mildly upset Canadians on your hands, though. Plus, they have free healthcare, meaning they don't mind getting roughed up. (Side note: don't do this.)

Bottom: A game as thoroughly frustrating as it is infuriating. Also, it's a little fun.

"Come with me. It's time to make a living."

Ziggy Gruber was only eight when this commandment was issued from his grandfather, Max. Max tossed his grandson an apron, and a Deli Man was born. Kosher Jewish delicatessens are a slowly disappearing breed. Growing up in his family's New York delis, Ziggy's youth was spent speaking Yiddish behind deli counters with Eastern European Jews like his grandfather, who moved to America from Budapest at sixteen. Old Country transplants who managed to escape the conflict and violence generally relied on three things to persevere: food, family, and humor.

As a child, Ziggy was immersed in tradition, learning the ropes of deli life from his uncles, father, and grandfather, all of whom either owned, operated, or worked in kosher delis in the New York

A Glossary of Useful Yiddish Words:

Haimish–cozy or comforting. "This matzo ball soup is haimish; it's like my bubi's."

Kvetch–to whine or complain. "Yes, waiter, I gotta' say the soup is cold," kvetched Lenny.

Mensch–a real good guy. "That Sarah, she married a real mensch."

Meshuggeneh–one who is crazy, wild, or insane. "Oy, my meshuggeneh nephew rides a motorcycle."

Nosh–to eat, or to to nibble just a little bit. "I'm not too hungry; I'll get a blintz to nosh on."

Tuches–your buttocks. "Sit your tuches down and eat!"

Left: It's a proper New York deli, so feel free to say "Fughedaboutit" and "You talkin' to me?" with aplomb.

Right: This is half a sandwich off the lunch menu. Regular-sized sandwiches here are the size of a toddler.

area. His grandpa Max opened Broadway Street's first deli in 1927 with his brothers in-law, where people like Groucho Marx and Milton Berle came to nosh on Old World classics like goulash and gefilte fish.

Nowadays, Ziggy Gruber operates what he considers the best deli in America, and diners would be hard pressed to argue. Gigantic sandwiches with clever names like the Fiddler on the Roof of Your Mouth and Brisky Business capable of feeding small villages make up a menu of more than two hundred items. New York cheesecake is one of the many dessert options inside the big cooler up front, while traditional Jewish foods like blintzes and stuffed cabbage are freshly made in house.

Like any good deli, there is also smoked fish.

Gruber flies in smoked fish daily from a purveyor in Brooklyn, and everything is hand sliced by skilled professionals. Few things on this planet are as satisfying to members of the Tribe than plates of lox, the smoked, sliced salmon generally served with bagels and a schmear of cream cheese.

When sick, Kenny and Ziggy's offers one of the city's best bowls of matzo ball soup, otherwise known as Jewish penicillin. Springy, spongy little orbs of goodness float in a chicken broth handsomely seasoned and cooked with rendered chicken fat known as schmaltz, a foundational ingredient of Jewish home cooking.

For all of his adherence and advocacy to deli traditions, Kenny Gruber really just wants to see people happy. Jews are a hearty folk, and their food is indicative of this. Dining in is pricey, but like any home cooked meal, it's best shared.

2327 Post Oak Boulevard
Houston, TX 77056
713-871-8883, kennyandziggys.com

Left: If a place calls itself a deli but doesn't serve Dr. Brown's, it's not a deli.

Right: Matzo ball soup, deconstructed. It will cure what ails you, unless what ails you is like, flesh-eating bacteria or something awful. In that case, see a doctor.

BARBECUE INN

Amanda Medsger is a Houston-based artist and stylist who works with some of the city's best chefs and restaurants. She styles photoshoots for openings, menus, and cookbooks. She designs incredible homes, bars, and restaurant interiors throughout Houston. Working with restaurants naturally involves being around—and eating—plenty of amazing food. When asked about her favorite fried chicken spot, however, her response was without hesitation.

"Go to Barbecue Inn and get their fried chicken," she said.

This may seem incongruous, like ordering a burger from an Italian restaurant, but rest assured she is totally, completely right. Every order is made from scratch, meaning wait times can be twenty to twenty-five minutes before giant servings of fried chicken are delivered to the table by the no-nonsense waitstaff.

(Side note: do not give the waitresses any guff. They will not abide an attitude. Charming and sweet, these old school servers wield a sass crisper than the battered chicken they serve.)

Opened in 1946—just one year after World War II ended—by Louis Skrehot and his wife Nell, not much has changed other than the prices in the ensuing seventy-two years inside Barbecue Inn. Originally, only beer and barbecue were served.

They still are, but the menu has expanded over the years to include all the down-home classics. Fan favorites like the fried shrimp and catfish will put a smile on any seafood lover's face, and the chicken fried steak, smothered in homemade cream gravy, is a classic example of the Texas staple dish. Round, lean beef steaks get pounded thin then floured, battered, and fried in butter on a griddle or tossed wholesale into a deep fryer. The end result is brittle crust clinging like gift wrapping to the fork-tender meat within.

Top Left: They like brown a lot, evidenced by the sign out front.

Top Right: This gentleman has the right idea: fried chicken for lunch.

Bottom Left: Chicken close up.

Barecue Inn's actual barbecue is serviceable, but the chicken stands out in a town that takes deep fried food very seriously. Frying chicken is an art form, and whatever secret ingredients or techniques the Skrehot family members employ certainly make their version of this classic dish worthy of hanging in a frame at the museum of fried chicken, if such a thing exists.

Residents of the Greater Oaks area in North Houston have been coming to eat at Barbecue Inn for generations. Still family owned, it's been serving regulars for so long that the kids are now parents and grandparents, bringing their own broods to cure cravings for homemade fried foods and ribs.

116 West Crosstimbers Street
Houston, TX 77018
713-695-8112, thebarbecueinn.com

VOODOO QUEEN DAIQUIRI DIVE

When a bar puts the word 'dive' right into its name there is usually one of two ways people react: scorn or interest.

Many find the notion of a dive bar unacceptable. Dim lighting competes with the dingy bathrooms and cigarette smoke clouds streaming in from outdoor patios. Dives play loud music and quite often the bartenders can be gruff.

But if you're anything like me, all that sounds great.

Thankfully Voodoo Queen is a bit of a compromise. It's nowhere as dive-y as the name would suggest. It definitely checks the boxes of dim lighting and smoky patios, but service is friendly and the music isn't played so loud as to make conversation impossible. All the vintage beer ads, neon lighting, and televisions brighten up the spartan interior. In fact, strip away the trappings of a bar and it's pretty much just a warehouse. It isn't as though they didn't warn everybody: because again, 'dive' is in the name. So is 'daiquiri,' which is what they do best.

Voodoo Queen's daiquiri list is massive, with frozen blends swirling about in mixing machines, hand-blended drinks with fresh fruit and rum, and a knockout concoction called the Bends. Described as a "box of banana creamsicles [strapped] to a torpedo and shot into a pirate ship full of rum and fireworks," customers are limited to three of these particularly strong libations.

There is no phone number, and yes the website really is damngoodfoodcoldassbeer.com. You know, 'cause they have damn good food and cold ass beers. Dot com.

Left: The Wipe Out, a watermelon flavored frozen drink with a floater of pure grain alcohol.

Middle Left: Shrimp po'boy, dressed with lettuce, tomato, pickles, and house mayo.

Middle Right: Drink menu. They also have a load of cans, bottles, and draft beer.

Right: Frozen blended daiquiri with a spicy straw coated in chili and lime seasoning for an added level of fun.

Frozen drinks can be mixed, too, and there is a menu of suggested combinations. Floaters of liquor can be added to any drink, sucked up into plastic syringes and inserted into the viscous frozen concoctions.

The extra shots of booze will slowly seep into the drink, or you can dance with the devil like a jive turkey and squeeze the whole shooter in.

Places like this are everywhere in New Orleans, and most of them have Everclear in the drinks, the grain alcohol strong enough to start a car engine. At Voodoo Queen, the frozen mixing machines and brightly colored, extra boozy slushies are the same basic idea and execution.

Keeping to the Crescent City concept, Voodoo Queen serves a limited food menu primarily of fried fare like po'boys and shrimp baskets. Po'boys here pay faithful homage to the original, with all the fixings and French bread crust anyone would need. Located in a soon-to-be gentrified East Downtown, Voodoo Queen is well worthy of a visit or three.

322 Milby Street
Houston, TX 77003
damngoodfoodcoldassbeer.com

HMart isn't a Houston-based business, though there are two stores in town.

A chain of Asian supermarkets with over sixty locations in major U.S. cities, H Mart is headquartered in New Jersey. It's a food lover's dream. The Bellaire location has affordable, high quality products, a food court, and cuts of sushi-grade fish.

Even if there's barely any time for a visit, at least go to the candy aisle. It's worth a trip on its own. Shelf after shelf of confections, chocolates, and candies are in stock from all across Asia. Get the Green Tea Kit Kats if they're in stock.

On the first Saturday of every month, H Mart has their chefs break down a whole bluefin tuna, and it's open to the public. Shoppers can get the fresh cuts right from the fish. Fresh tuna with a little soy sauce is one of the more delicious bites of food on Earth. Shoppers can get the tuna wrapped up to take home, as well. It is actually quite a rare thing to have an opportunity to source sushi. To know first-hand where the fish was caught, butchered, and sold isn't common for consumers.

In Asia, vendors selling inferior product don't last; the market is too discerning. H Mart understands that quality breeds loyalty. It's always busy, and the products are consistently high quality. H Mart demonstrates this ideal, and clearly puts effort into maintaining it. H mart's variety and diversity offered is unparalleled, and exploring it is a must.

1302 Blalock Road
Houston, TX 77055
713-468-0606, hmart.com

9896 Bellaire Boulevard
Houston, TX 77036
713-270-1110

Top Left: Fresh kimchi.

Top Right: Whole cuts of sushi-grade salmon; sashimi plate. It's affordable and excellent quality.

Bottom Left: Chinese barbeque.

Bottom Right: The aforementioned candy aisle. Wisely, they have bulk toothbrush packages every few inches between the many shelves of sweets.

ANVIL BAR AND REFUGE

To say the bartenders at Anvil are meticulous would be fair. It would also be a monumental understatement.

Every bartender at this trendy and upscale cocktail bar undergoes a stringent training program culminating in a blind taste test of fifty spirits. Trainees must get forty-seven correct to pass. This doesn't include Anvil's additional requirement: memorization of THE 100 LIST. It's Anvil's classic cocktail collection, the threshold of entry each bartender must know by heart.

Seasonal menus introduce new, exciting flavors, but the original concoctions served at this award-winning establishment have exerted immense influence over Houston's cocktail culture. Former employees have brought their expertise to bear, opening bars and curating drink menus all over the world.

"Christopher Columbus Was an Asshole" is Anvil's annual "tribute" to the famed explorer's numerous "contributions" to the world. A themed menu of special cocktails provides enlightening details to Columbus's decidedly heinous exploits. Historical accounts of Columbus's various acts of murder, enslavement of native peoples, genocide, theft, and general immorality are laid bare.

The event is held each Columbus Day, obviously. Generally speaking, learning and drinking aren't often associated with one another, but Anvil enjoys giving patrons such an important opportunity.

As the event description explains: "Every once in a while, a little history and cocktails is a good thing."

A highly focused food menu provides sustenance for the rigorous duties of imbibing. Anvil serves bar snacks like charcuterie boards, pretzels, and Scotch eggs, the heart attack snack of choice. Wine and beer are carefully selected, but cocktails are king. Dimly lit inside, crowds tend to converge on weekends and for busy weeknight happy hours, where networking is easily facilitated via strong drinks and excellent service.

Owner and Houstonian Bobby Heugel is somewhat of a local celebrity. He and his original business partner built out Anvil's interior almost entirely by themselves, rejuvenating the historic building which originally housed a tire shop in the late 1950s. It was never Heugel's intention to become the face of Houston's bar scene, but such a fate is difficult to avoid for a multiple time James Beard nominee running one of the best bars in America—if not the world—according to *Esquire*, *GQ*, and *Southern Living*, to name a few.

Cocktails like boozy Manhattans are diligently prepared, but explore deeper into the expansive selection of handmade drinks to truly get a feel for Anvil's creativity. "The Brave," which Heugel worked for a full year on before the bar opened, has been a mainstay on the shifting menus ever since. A tantalizing blend of mezcal, tequila, liqueurs, and bitters, this tart, smoky tonic won't necessarily induce acts of heroism, as the name suggests. It will, however, take the edge off long days in the office.

Be ready to practice patience. Each cocktail is carefully mixed, poured, and garnished individually.

When busy, bartenders shift into machine-like efficiency, shaking, stirring, and serving some of the finest cocktails in town. Regardless of preference, Anvil has the right drink for everyone.

Just drink responsibly.

1424 Westheimer Road
Houston, TX 77006
713-523-1622, anvilhouston.com

BOMBAY PIZZA COMPANY

Viral Patel was managing a now-defunct Italian restaurant for almost 12 years before opening Bombay Pizza in 2009 with his mother Sonali. Their concept was fusing Italian flavors with the Indian spices he'd grown up eating as a child

On a pre-launch trip to India, American-born Viral spent his time wisely, expanding and refining his already broad knowledge of traditional Indian cooking. With his new skills and experience in hand, he returned home to Houston and developed a menu that will surprise diners. This mother-son team was able to fashion a wholly new kind of food, crafting a mix of complex and accessible.

To the uninitiated, many of Bombay's pizza toppings would seem a hard sell, but the reality is anything but. The tastes are at once oddly familiar and amazingly unusual. Razor-thin sesame crusts are perfect vessels for pizzas possessing names with as much flavor as the food—like the Gateway to India, with tandoori chicken, crab meat, artichoke hearts, provolone, mozzarella and cilantro-mint chutney in place of the traditional red sauce. Bombay's menu also offers naan rolls, salads, and chili-garlic ranch for dipping purposes. Classic Italian-American dishes like chicken parm and fettuccine alfredo are also available for more circumspect guests.

Mo Rocca, the humorist, writer, and television personality featured the Gateway to India on an episode of Food Network's show *The Best Thing I Ever Ate*, calling it the "Mother Teresa" of pizzas.

While they may never be canonized, Bombay Pizza Company is nevertheless worthy of praise.

914 South Main Street, #105
Houston, TX 77002
713-654-4444, bombaypizzaco.com

Left: Close-up of the Thai red curry pizza. It's fan-freaking-tastic.

Middle: Lots of unique, non-traditional toppings for your 'za.

Right: Sign outside the main location.

LANKFORD GROCERY

Lankford Grocery is pretty cut and dry. It is uncomplicated, inauspicious, and blessedly unaware of what those terms mean when it comes to lovingly handmade food. Open at 7 a.m. to serve a bang-up breakfast, Lankford also closes at 3 p.m.

Lunch crowds can be packed to the point of chaotic and parking kind of sucks. The surrounding Fourth Ward streets are dilapidated, and full of potholes. There appears to be near-constant need for construction in the area.

Service can be rushed. Among the veteran staff, there is little tolerance for any ballyhoo, hijinks, or tomfoolery from their customers: no, not one bit. It is altogether too cramped inside.

Ever homey, always crowded, and a bit run down—it has character.

Despite all of this, Lankford Grocery has outlasted the evolving turmoil experienced by most of the area for almost eighty years. Mostly, this is because of their hamburgers. Serving an all-American line up of belt-busting, beefy two-handers, Lankford has earned local love and national acclaim. Even meat damp Guy Fieri, the unrivaled king of limp one-liners and bleach-blonde hair spikes, loves Lankford Grocery. Although it isn't a drive in, it most definitely is a dive and diner.

Truthfully, the weekend morning biscuits and gravy special would be enough to keep any place afloat. Fans of the daily rotation of famous lunch specials are fiercely loyal, too. The specials don't really change.

> Notable events from 1937: Amelia Earhart disappeared, Daffy Duck premiered, the Hindenburg exploded, *Snow White and the Seven Dwarves* premiered, *The Hobbit* was published, future President Ronald Reagan made his film debut in *Love Is on the Air*, the Golden Gate Bridge opened, the Massacre at Nanking occurred, Lankford Grocery opened.

Top Left: Burger with bacon and all the fixins'.

Top Right: Look for the house with the two greatest flags in the world.

Bottom Left: Lankford Grocery sign.

Solace can be found in the cheesy beef enchiladas or chicken fried steak. As their menu states, "We have nothing small, nothing fast, and nothing healthy."

Take the Grim Burger, for instance. A half-pound beef patty is topped with a hefty scoop of macaroni and cheese, bacon, jalapeños, and a fried egg. Your heart may stop, but it will nonetheless be a delicious demise. Lankford's other burgers can be somewhat experimental but always follow familiar routes, like the Frito pie burger, wasabi burger, and quesadilla burger. For those considering themselves chiliheads, the firehouse burger is an admirable test, adorned with a sauce made from habaneros grown out back, cayenne butter, and jalapeños.

Eydie Prior has run Lankford masterfully, taking over from her folks who opened the place all those years ago. It can be hot and busy, but if it isn't one of Houston's best burgers then I'm a Dallas Cowboys fan.

Lankford remains cash only, which is slightly disappointing. But not as disappointing as the Dallas Cowboys.

88 Dennis Street
Houston, TX 77006
713-522-9555

CLEBURNE CAFETERIA

Easily the best way to understand the family behind Cleburne Cafeteria is by spending some time examining the photographs and artwork filling the restaurant's walls. About seventy years of family photos show the story of a devoted and loving family.

Devoted to each other always.

Nick Mickelis came to America to make a life for his family. Rather, for the family he would have. He met his wife, Pat, a photographer, when his mother asked him for pictures of his new life in America. Pat liked Nick, and she would visit him at the barbecue restaurant he'd scraped and saved to purchase after years of working for his brother. He couldn't afford any kind of wallpaper or fancy decorations, so he painted murals in the place himself, ever the artist at heart. Pat would come to Nick's restaurant for coffee. She enjoyed watching Nick paint the walls when he wasn't serving customers or cooking. Pat and Nick married in Houston at the Annunciation Greek Orthodox Cathedral.

Originally, Cleburne Cafeteria was opened in 1941, but the Mikelis family bought it from the previous owners. A lot has happened since then, both as a restaurant and a family. Nick and Pat raised their kids above Cleburne, in a house full of trapdoors and secret bolt holes; it used to be a speakeasy before it became a restaurant. Their kids have had kids, and the restaurant continues to grow, despite burning to the ground twice and closures during some of the city's catastrophic flooding.

Cleburne still serves its well-made, throwback cafeteria food like fried catfish, chicken-fried chicken, and roast beef. It's the South, which means things are fried and there's lots of it, served out on trays to the many hungry diners patronizing Cleburne each day.

This is absolutely true at Cleburne Cafeteria, where the portions of everything are gargantuan. Adding one slice of cake or pie for dessert nearly requires an extra set of hands because of the size.

Top Left: Pie, pie, and more pie.

Top Right: A full tray of Cleburne's classic cafeteria food.

Bottom Left: A small selection of steaks, always cooked to order.

Bottom Right: Massive hunks of cake, as well. Photos by Oliver Rufio Fieriro.

Honestly, a single slice of cake is so outrageously large, it necessitates sharing. Cleburne's cakes are as big as everything else served, and the standout chocolate and strawberry slices nearly necessitate a tray of their own. One may be hesitant to indulge in dessert, but Cleburnes Cafeteria is not the place for such sentiment. It's worth the guilt.

Unfortunately, this may lead to some slight maternal resentment. Mom never made it this good.

3606 Bissonnet Street
Houston, TX 77005
713-667-2386, cleburnecafeteria.com

AL QUICK STOP

Evolutionary psychology provides real insight for deciphering human behaviors. As a species, humans are not particularly good at evaluating new experiences. While certainly useful, our innate tendency of forming immediate snap judgements remains antithetical to finding joy in new experiences.

Evidence of this human tendency for snap-judgment is easily observed by the simple fact that so many Houstonians don't know about AL Quick Stop, but AL's might have Houston's best falafel. It's always made to order, crispy, and utterly, amazingly devoid of the usual greasiness from any fry oil. The deep-fried disks of ground chickpea are topped with a handful of fresh herbs for a bright, clean flavor. Definitely adorn the falafel with AL's house-made tahini and chunky hot sauce for added depth. Expanded social media presence brought about by popular delivery apps like UberEats and DoorDash allowed AL's to fully flourish, finding firm footing in Houston for good.

It's a little bit run-down and cramped, but phenomenal food elevates the humble aspects of a café within a convenience store to new heights. Tightly packed shelves occupy most of the store's available floor space, and the functional menu also has gyros and kabobs in addition to classic Mexican and American favorites like tacos and burgers. Over to the side is a walk-up food counter, manned by members of the family and their dedicated staff. In the very back is a tiny dining area. Nevertheless, it all comes together in a curiously sensible manner..

AL Quick Stop is exactly itself, without frills, ostentation, or presumption.

AL means "the" in Arabic, and this small, family-run bodega prides itself on being not just a quick stop, but 'The' Quick Stop in the Hyde Park area of Montrose. This pride is not without merit, either.

Top Left: Just part of the large menu on offer. Delivery services keep this corner store humming late into the night. Falafel and gyros zip out the door for delivery to those of us too lazy to leave our couches. Let's take a moment to recognize the delivery drivers of the world. Thank you. You matter.

Top Right: Gyro meat rotating on the spit.

Bottom Left: Look for the sky-blue paint job and hookah. (Side note: actually, there isn't hookah available at AL's.)

Bottom Right: Best falafel in Houston.

Opened in 1991 as a friendly corner store, most patrons personify the place as 'Al's,' though no such person exists. For too long, though, potential customers didn't really know about the quality cuisine on offer. Any remaining cognitive biases from the unassuming aesthetics disappear after one taste of their falafel, effectively supplanting any preconceived notion about eating at convenience stores adjacent to dive bars. There's an odd collection of home goods, do-rags, snacks, beer, and wine. Somehow, it all makes perfect sense in the end. Simply put, this is one of those places people drive by every day but just never stop at. That's definitely a huge mistake.

Huge.

2002 Waugh Drive
Houston, TX 77006

CONSERVATORY

Malls were important to teenagers growing up in suburban America during the 1980s and 1990s.

Kids lacked cars and credit cards, making malls perfect places for doing dumb things. With a little luck and minor planning, saving enough lunch money throughout the week bought Orange Julius or stupid t-shirts from Spencer's Gifts.

Outside of going to the mall, there wasn't much else to do for kids too young for a driver's license.

Movie theaters were an option, but no-talking rules run antithetical to teenage conduct. Sure, it's good gossip learning who hooked up during whatever Adam Sandler movie was playing, but movies are expensive and static. Malls circumvented pricey concessions and requisite silence.

At mall food courts everything is copacetic.

Exhausted moms eat froyo and rock their screaming children. Families share oversized cinnamon rolls at four in the afternoon. Old men meet for coffee before shops open, early enough to make meandering laps around the empty mall.

Perhaps this is why modern food halls are so successful. To adults, restaurants are like the movies: we can't be loud because there's a sense of decorum. Dress codes and pushy servers mean rules. Conservatory offers a distinct freedom from such restraints. Chef-driven food courts have become more common in recent years, catering to a discerning clientele seeking expansive, gourmet dining options.

It's the kind of place everyone wants in their neighborhood. The thing is, they just don't know it yet.

Even with the seemingly endless construction and bustle of Downtown, descending into Conservatory provides guests a subterranean urban oasis, an escape from the commerce, traffic, and

Great pho from the Pho Stop.

the always stifling Houston heat. Vendors occasionally rotate, but the full-service wine bar and draft beer bar don't. Whether seeking a quick lunch or a full meal, Conservatory's variety is sure to please. On Fridays and Saturdays, Conservatory stays open until 3 a.m., likely catering to the revelers emerging from the numerous drinking establishments close by.

Food halls like Conservatory are ideal late night spots, in fact. Where else can someone get pizza, pho, or a reuben at two in the morning?

Although the food options rotate in new blood, there are plenty of fine choices ranging from barbecue to sandwiches to sweet treats and pizza. It's everything a food court should be and then some, as well as a perfect meeting point to bar hop around the trendy bars close by in Downtown.

1010 Prairie Street
Houston, TX 77002
832-919-8382, conservatoryhtx.com

STAR PIZZA

There is something to be said about controversy. Biggie vs. Tupac. Elvis vs. the Beatles.

Or even something as primal and rudimentary as apples or bananas. Maybe Raffi had it right: it's not apples or bananas, but apples and bananas. These two fruits are far from the only controversy when it comes to food. People get quite touchy when it comes to how they eat, and positively petulant when it comes to how others eat.

Put ketchup on a hot dog in Chicago and see what happens. Or, better yet, insult the idea of Chicago style deep dish. I mean, really get in there and talk trash about deep dish and see how well it goes.

It's a casserole! It's a big, soupy mess! You can't fold it! It takes fifty minutes!

It is often said there is no such thing as bad publicity. When it comes to food, it's no surprise to see this occur regularly as well.

In part, such controversy is responsible for Star Pizza's success. One of Houston's original purveyors of Chicago deep dish, with the option for whole wheat crusts, Star has been a pillar of the local pizza scene since owners Hank and Marilyn Zwirek opened in 1976, right off the Southwest Freeway. Between the outstretched arms of Shepherd and Greenbriar, the original Star sits on a bulbous elbow of land requiring some clever navigation for first timers.

Look, deep dish gets a bad rap. Done poorly, deep dish is an undercooked, soggy casserole. The soaking moisture from sauce and ingredients and blackened exterior often yields a soupy and disappointing interior. Done correctly, deep dish is merely a slightly thicker crust filled with layers of cheese, sauce, and meat. Thicker crust lends some density and support to the fillings, yet is still cooked until it's crunchable. Star does Chicago deep dish justice.

Left: Pizza.

Top Right: Star's Heights Location at night.

Bottom Right: Star's original location on Norfolk.

A second location in the Heights succeeded, but plans were made in 1999 to pull up stakes and renovate a new Star Pizza at Washington and Waugh. Apparently, pizza acumen begets real estate savvy. The move was prescient of the massive retail, commercial, and residential growth that has since occurred since.

One thing Houstonians can all agree on is a good buffet. Weekday lunch is all-you-can-eat buffet at Star Pizza, with a plentiful salad bar, breadsticks, and fresh pies delivered regularly. Tea or soda is also included, of course.

2111 Norfolk Street
Houston, TX 77098
713-523-0800, starpizza.net

DOLLAR HOT DOG NIGHT AT MINUTE MAID PARK

Sergeant Matthew Austin Gaines is an American Hero. A Combat Medic in the United States Army from 2004–2009, Sergeant Gaines served two tours of duty in Iraq.

"Twelve months each. Two years of my life," he adds, affecting the typically macabre humor of veterans.

He's deserving of our admiration and respect, though he generally prefers to make things about everyone else. While the rest of his friends were being dumb teenagers in college, Sergeant Gaines signed up to serve his country.

It wasn't fun. It wasn't pretty. It was war.

Besides his family, Sergeant Gaines has two other true loves in life: Houston sports and food. So naturally, he loves attending any Astros games on Dollar Hot Dog Night at Minute Maid Park. Fans can get hot dogs for just $1 every Tuesday during home games. There's no limit, either. Sponsored by Nolan Ryan Beef, the promotion is an easy, fun way to take the family to a ball game.

Hot dogs are America. Tubes of processed meat encased in white bread mean freedom. Freedom to eat in a terrible and unhealthy manner but also the freedom to smother a hot dog with whatever condiments one so desires. Luckily, the condiments—like napkins—are free, so be liberal with the toppings. Pair the dogs with some Saint Arnold's craft beer, which has multiple locations around the ballpark with ample of options and variety.

In some ways, the Dollar Hot Dog promotion is a service to the fans.

During the lean years, when the Astros lost 100 games for two consecutive seasons, Dollar Hot Dog Nights were usually the only games that approached capacity crowds. Baseball can be hard

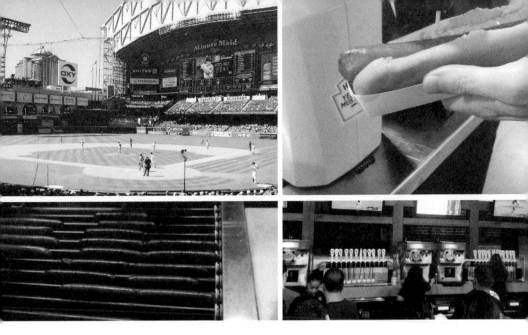

Top Left: Minute Maid is one of the best ballparks in the majors, hands down.

Top Right: Like napkins, condiments are free and plentiful, so load it on up.

Bottom Left: Rolling wieners, the only way to cook a ballpark hot dog.

Bottom Right: Saint Arnold's has a bar on the first level of Minute Maid, serving a big selection of their famous Houston craft brew.

enough to watch for casual fans, so when a team is truly bad it is practically torture, even for diehards.

The Astros have been one of the best teams in baseball over the last few years, which totally helps.

Winning the World Series during the 2017-2018 season went even further toward ensuring fans were in seats the following year. Everybody loves winners; most everybody loves wieners, as well. Yet, even when the Astros were decidedly not good, the hot dogs made do. The event generated revenue, of course, but it also showed fans appreciation despite poor production on the field.

On the first Dollar Hot Dog Night of 2018, fans consumed 43,000 hot dogs.

Sergeant Matthew Austin Gaines ate twelve of the dogs by himself.

501 Crawford Street
Houston, TX 77002
713-259-8000, houston.astros.mlb.com

HAY MERCHANT

When Hurricane Harvey struck Houston in 2017, the city shut down. Roads flooded. Many homes were lost, and many lives were taken. Emerging from catastrophe shows what the city is capable of. Friends, neighbors, and strangers mingled, grieved, and persevered.

It was a tragedy of immeasurable impact, yet at the same time brought Houstonians together in common cause. Local restaurants didn't escape the carnage. Many had to close for repairs, and some shuttered permanently. Around town, restaurants able to open after Harveys were beacons of hope.

Shortly after the storm, the Hay Merchant invited guests in, serving whatever they could. The semblance of normalcy, albeit momentarily, was a gift. My wife and I walked on over there from our nearby apartment. It was one of the best meals of our lives. It wasn't that the food was good (it was), or beer helped us unwind (it did).

Sometimes, food is more than sustenance. It is community and comfort. There was an esprit de corps, as guests bonded over shared experiences of making it through one of the worst events Houston ever endured.

And endure we did.

Chris Shepherd opened the Hay Merchant with partners Bobby Heugel and Kevin Floyd in 2012, planning to pair a beer bar with great food for the neighborhood. Today, it's one of the best places to drink beer in the country.

Shepherd, arguably the most recognizable face in Houston's food scene, with television appearances alongside luminaries like David Chang and the late Anthony Bourdain, crafts the menu. Floyd, a beer guru, oversees diverse tap selections and encyclopedic beer lists, offering different rare cask and bottle varietals. Heugel left

Top Left: The famous Korean braised goat and dumplings.

Top Right: Family-style chicken-fried steak, enough for two or three people.

Bottom Left: Sundays are Fried Chicken Night. Photo by the Kellys.

Bottom Right: The cease and desist with fries.

the business, but the focus on gourmet food and craft beer remains steadfast.

Recent expansion into cocktails caters to non-beer drinkers, and Shepherd continually develops new food. Shepherd strives to reflect Houston's diversity, featuring Asian-inspirations, classic pub food, and family-style meals. Korean braised goat and dumplings, wings, and sweet, spicy pig ears are menu staples. There is also the Cease and Desist burger.

Originally called the "Double Double," a cease and desist order from California chain In-N-Out forced the team to re-brand. With a sardonic twist honoring the legal kerfuffle, the Cease and Desist was christened anew. Shepherd's mom-inspired lasagna and roasted, whole pig heads can feed entire tables—or at least one drunk guy.

It is a place to rest both elbows, eat well, and relax.

1100 Westheimer Road

Houston, TX 77006

713-528-9805, haymerchant.com

FRANK'S PIZZA AND BACKYARD

A long-standing fixture of the Houston Downtown community, Frank's Pizza is far more than a pizza shop. Renowned as a late-night haven for hungry Astros and Rockets fans seeking post-game grub, the area's development and expansion likewise impacted Frank's patronage and presence. For many years, though, Frank's was a beacon in an after-hours dead zone.

Downtown used to be quiet at night, especially during the week. Restaurant hours there followed a 9 to 5 schedule. As skyscrapers emptied of all but the most committed corporate cronies, nearby restaurants followed suit. Only a few historic bars that have seemingly been around forever like La Carafe and Warren's Inn regularly provided Frank's with customers. Downtown was generally bereft of much action once the sun sank.

Regular events at Market Square Park and numerous new bars, hotels, and apartments have changed the landscape of this urban playground. Also, a popular music festival, staged by Free Press Houston every December called Day for Night, ensures that Frank's has non-stop lines of raucous, ravenous revelers, many of whom are under the influence of far more than hunger pangs.

Today, expansion into a neighboring lot, purchased by owners Deborah and Eddie Love in 2010, has produced Frank's Backyard,

> Most places Downtown were totally inaccessible during Hurricane Harvey, but Frank's loyal employees went above and beyond in giving back. First Responders had put out a call for food from anyone who could help, and Frank's went into action, cooking up an army's worth of their food to personally deliver to the heroic response workers.

Left: Frank's iconic signage in Downtown Houston.
Right: Extra-large pizzas sold by the slice.

an open-air bar with cocktails and forty-eight taps offering a casual compliment to the busy scene next door. Food can be delivered or walked over after ordering, but only food from Frank's Pizza is allowed. Beer and wine are served at each adjacent location, but the hard stuff is exclusively at Frank's Backyard.

Frank's Pizza is cramped and narrow, reminiscent of a shotgun-style row house, deeper by far than it is wide. Pizza by the slice is Frank's forte. Slices are very large, lines go fast, and toppings run the traditional gamut of plain cheese, pepperoni, or a fully loaded supreme. The crust is thin and crispy, and the individual slices themselves are fairly large. Whole pies can be custom ordered, as can oven-toasted sandwiches and wings.

Very limited seating is available along the walls. Seats can be found up front and in a second-floor loft, yet there's no shame eating on the curb—simply lean forward to avoid messy shirts.

It's a perfect slice, and perfectly egalitarian. Despite busy crowds, pizza-by-the-slice is always fresh and served sans judgement. Regardless of state or status Frank's Pizza produces classic pies—a memorable, precise blend of filling, familiar, and foldable.

And for sure delicious.

417 Travis Street
Houston, TX 77002
frankspizza.com

The best time to visit Hugo's is for Sunday brunch. Hear me out. First off, it's a great value. A flat fee gets diners a unique opportunity: Hugo's endless brunch buffet, an open invitation to truly test the limits of better judgement. Inner turmoil can be set aside; embrace the gluttony.

Another plate is a great idea. No, one piece of tres leches is assuredly not enough—that kind of thing. Simply put, the food is marvelous. Seating is comfortable and relaxed. Staff members function as a singular, formidable unit. Every server, manager, busser, and kitchen member makes the monumental task of serving endless Sunday Brunch to one of America's most food-centric cities look downright easy.

As far as rags-to-riches tales go, Hugo Ortega's life story is far from ordinary. Ordinary doesn't win James Beard Awards. Ordinary doesn't produce the flavors, passion, and drive that make Ortega's restaurants so immensely popular. Thankfully, Chef Ortega is anything but ordinary.

Immigration, one of America's great traditions, brought Chef Ortega to Houston in 1984. Born in Mexico City, he arrived with nothing in his pocket and little in the way of prospects or contacts. He began working odd jobs to make ends meet, cleaning office buildings and washing dishes at a nightclub. Everything changed when Ortega became a dishwasher at Backstreet Cafe.

By 1993, Hugo Ortega was Executive Chef at Backstreet Cafe and a culinary school graduate. Most importantly he married Tracy Vaught, the restaurant's owner, giving the term 'business partners' a whole new meaning.

Together, the duo's H-Town Restaurant Group introduced Hugo's in 2002, Caracol in 2013, and Xochi in 2017. Caracol serves mainly seafood, drawing inspiration from Mexico's sixteen coastal

Top Left: Butternut squash soup.

Top Middle: Hugo's dessert menu is worth a thorough exploration. Or, just attend Hugo's Sunday brunch and enjoy the Mexican hot chocolate, churros, cakes, cookies, and a million other confections worth sampling.

Right: Want any cocktail with your chili?

Bottom: Roasted root vegetable dish; amazingly flavorful.

states. Xochi pays homage to Oaxaca, with rich moles and maybe a grasshopper or two.

The second best time to visit Hugo's is during Houston Restaurant Weeks (HRW). Each year HRW raises money for the Houston Food Bank. Restaurants provide prix-fixe menus with multiple courses, and Hugo's goes all out.

Usually three or four menus are available, focused around each course's pairing with a particular drink, like red wine varietals or cocktails. Hugo's regularly creates stellar vegetarian dishes for their ever-evolving menus while the bar program is as successful as it is ambitious.

The third best time to eat at Hugo's is right now, maybe for a cocktail at the bar with a tasty late night snack.

They'd love to see you.

1600 Westheimer Road
Houston, TX 77006
713-524-7744, hugosrestaurant.net

RIVA'S ITALIAN RESTAURANT

How does one explain the inexplicable?

Encapsulating Riva's is like attempting to define color. In short, Riva's defies any and all explanation.

It challenges expectations, yet remains a perfectly charming host to anyone who walks in.

Seeking younger, livelier clientele, brothers/owners Mike and Joe Sibouyeh moved their original location to a Montrose bungalow in 1996. Longtime champions of LGBTQIA+ causes, Riva's unabashedly embraces alternative lifestyles.

Riva's definitely is lively, particularly during Sunday brunches, which take on a celebratory air. Brunch crowds bounce to techno soundtracks while downing mimosas and fresh melon slices.

Many patrons take the "bottomless" modifier as a direct challenge. That's just smart consumerism. No pursuit is more meaningful than any individual, regardless of lifestyle, getting their dime's worth in endless drinks. That's just American.

Riva's Italian-American cuisine doesn't disappoint. Most entrees begin with soup and salad. Riva's lentil soup is rich, yet not heavy. Salads come undressed, but are served alongside jugs of ranch and Italian dressing. Use the little spoons and mix the two for a velvety, tangy contrast.

Cheesy, slightly sweet red sauce binds a scratch-made lasagna that requires a nap afterwards. The chicken mozzarella in creamy-carrot sauce requires two naps. A large menu and big portions guarantee patrons won't leave hungry, but meals are sometimes secondary. Experiencing Riva's in its wondrous glory alone is worth a trip.

It's nearly impossible to leave unhappy. Riva's staff turnover is practically non-existent. Joyful, fabulous servers flit around tables like beautiful lightning bugs, brightening guests with loving service

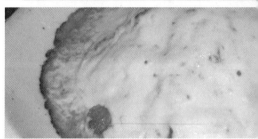

Top Left: Riva's staff are incredible—kind and so much fun.

Top Right: Just a random, stunningly beautiful woman having a Bloody Mary.

Bottom Left: They won't let guests endlessly mimosa without having something to eat. Fair warning: their mimosas are 90% champagne and 5% orange juice. The remaining 5% is love.

Bottom Right: Underneath all that cheese is a piece of lasagna, believe it or not.

and ebullient spirits. They care, and it shows. Visit Riva's once or twice and they'll probably remember. The next visit, you'll be greeted with smiles, hellos, and hugs. You'll be fed and treated like an equal.

Just like any friend should be.

117 Missouri Street
Houston, TX 77006
713-529-3450, rivasrestaurant.com

GOODNIGHT CHARLIE'S

True Texas honky-tonks are easy to spot, and signs are apparent at Goodnight Charlie's.

Basically, imagine John Travolta's movie *Urban Cowboy*, but a glossier and more refined version than the 1971 Houston bar where it was set. These country & western dance hall and bar hybrids are sparse in Houston nowadays, but are characterized by loud music, cold beer, cowboy hats, and tight jeans on the patrons parading about a rollicking dance floor. Everyone is a-whirling in two-step rhythm at Goodnight Charlie's, melding honky-tonk roots and country music with modern twists.

The name honors legendary Texas cattleman Charles Goodnight, a man known for inventing chuck wagons, forging trails, and fighting Indians. When Goodnight died at a spry ninety-three, he was perhaps the last relic of America's Wild West.

Goodnight Charlie's pays homage to tradition, but certainly makes alterations and improvements.

Sleek, beautifully designed and decorated interiors resemble an odd cross between hipster wine bar and an old, wooden barn. Shiny

Well into his 80s, Charles Goodnight began corresponding with a distant relative named Corinne Goodnight. Corinne was a nurse. She went to Charles Goodnight's bedside when he fell ill, nursing him slowly back to health. He became so healthy, in fact, that the two were married on his 91st birthday, making Corinne's legal name Corinne Goodnight Goodnight. They had a stillborn son one year later, shortly before Goodnight's death. Suffice it to say, Corinne was one hell of a nurse.

Top Left: Frozen mixed drinks. Be careful, though; they're strong.

Top Right: Charles Goodnight himself, fit as a fiddle and ready to party.

picnic tables inside and on the airy back patios are laid-back, open spaces for casual, early evening get-togethers and happy hours. Classic records from country stars like Merle Haggard, David Allen Coe, and Willie Nelson spin over the crisp sound system.

Nighttime brings in a much different crowd. Honky-tonks are generally crowded, rowdy places where boys and girls swing each other around by the arms. Local bands and touring acts take the stage nightly on weekends, providing down-home soundtracks for bootin', scootin', and boogyin'.

Chef Felipe Riccio curates a focused, eclectic menu, borrowing from traditional Mexican, Tex-Mex, and Southern cuisines. Born in Mexico City and raised in Veracruz, Chef Riccio has been cooking since high school.

"These flavors are familiar to me," he says, "because they are home." Tacos like mole verde with braised chicken are wrapped in handmade tortillas from Blanca Ramirez, lovingly known as the "Tortilla Angel" for her grace and skill.

Riccio moved to Houston at thirteen and has worked in premier kitchens all over the world ever since. Mentorship by master Sommelier and co-owner David Keck is ultimately what kept Riccio in town, however. After working kitchens in Houston, New York, and around Europe, he returned to his adopted home as chef/partner in Goodnight Hospitality, implementing his tremendous expertise in truly original ways.

Great food, service, and drinks make Goodnight Charlie's the place to gather with the folks who matter for some good times.

2531 Kuester Street
Houston, TX 77006
832-986-5151, goodnightcharlies.com

Top Left: Los mejores mariachis del mundo.

Top Right: Durros, a cloud-like fried wheat puff doused in hot sauce.

Bottom: Tacos. Some other tacos. And some even better tacos. They are all good, and I'll fight anyone who says otherwise Texas style, which means grain alcohol, blindfolds, and one crowbar thrown into a windowless room.

TEX CHICK PUERTO RICAN

"Do you know who that was?" the owner asked. "That was Carlos Beltrán."

He was a big guy; that's for sure, with bulging muscles and tree stumps for legs. But before I could say anything, the former outfielder and his Latin entourage had already piled into the large SUV waiting on them outside. It took him and two helpers to carry all of their Styrofoam takeout boxes into the truck.

Beltrán ordered enough of Tex Chick's family made, home-cooked meals to feed a small army or a clubhouse of hungry ball players looking for a taste of home. Beltrán, who hails from Puerto Rico, fell in love with Tex Chick during his legendary run with the Astros in 2004. He was a hero in 2004, bashing homers in five consecutive playoff appearances while notching fourteen RBIs during his twelve-game postseason.

Even though he left for greener pastures (and by that, I mean a lot of money) Beltrán would come back to Tex Chick every time he was in town for a series, according to the owner. He would always get plenty of extra for his teammates, too.

> Puerto Rico has still not recovered from the two hurricanes that battered the islands in 2017. There are still people without power, water, and sanitary products. It is always important to research charities carefully, as unfortunately there exist in our world people willing to fraudulently capitalize on the good will of their fellow man. However, there are numerous charitable foundations still working closely with the local government and residents to rebuild. Please consider donating. Regardless of politics, these are people who need our help.

Left: Carne guisada with rice, beans, and fried plantains.
Right: The outside of Tex Chick. Viva Puerto Rico.

It isn't hard to see why. Anyone who hasn't tried mofongo is seriously, seriously missing out. The same goes for Tex Chick's carne guisada and pechuga a la plancha.

Health food it is not, but delicious food it definitely is.

Beltrán was persona non grata after his departure from Houston. Fans thought he was greedy and selfish. It's easy as a fan to forget that ball players are human beings. They eat and sleep just like we do, and afterwards they poop like us, too. Also, ball players like money and providing for their families. Mostly, we are just jealous because they get to do it by playing sports better than us.

Luckily, the story has a happy ending.

Tex Chick is still serving fabulous, hand crafted meals out of their tiny restaurant off Fairview. It's still a mom-and-pop joint, surviving a fire and the ever-present pressures of the restaurant industry with charm and grace.

And for Carlos Beltrán?

Well, he returned to Houston twelve years later to play his final season with the Astros, helping to lead the team to its first World Series title in franchise history. While it remains uncertain how much Tex Chick's mofongo helped fuel the championship season, one can speculate it certainly didn't hurt.

712 ½ Fairview Street
Houston, TX 77006
713-528-4708

GOVINDA'S VEGETARIAN CUISINE

Nutrition is important, but far too many people do not wholly understand. Frankly, people don't want to know, like how seeing sausages are prepared makes it somewhat harder to eat one.

The result is we eat too much salt and sugar. We consume way too much meat. The average American will eat 222.22 pounds of red meat and poultry in 2018, according to the USDA. Not only is this practice unsustainable, but it's expensive and terribly harmful for the environment.

We should be motivated to fix some of the problems facing our world. However, one small thing we can do is to eat less meat. Plant-based diets are an emerging trend in the U.S., but societies the world over have long understood the advantages of vegetarianism.

About 30% of India is vegetarian, where the main religion is Hinduism. Hinduism doesn't absolutely, explicitly ban the consumption of animals, but most followers practicing vegetarianism do so because it aligns well with their true faith. In the *Tirukkural*, a collection of 7th century couplets, the basics of a virtuous life are laid out to the reader. In one such line, the poet-author Thiruvalluvar writes:

"How can he practice true compassion, who eats the flesh of an animal to fatten his own flesh?"

These cultures make a fair point, one that can be explored fully at Govinda's Vegetarian Cuisine. Attached to a beautiful Hindu temple and cultural center in the Heights, Govinda's serves some of the best vegetarian cuisine in Houston. Affordable and healthy, the all-you-can-eat lunch and dinner buffets have incredible variety. Govinda's

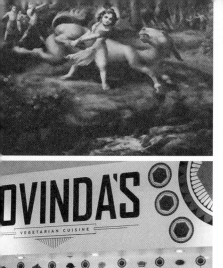

Top Left: Kill that Ass Demon! Kill him dead.

Top Right: Some more of the stunning artwork inside the temple.

Bottom Left: Listing many of the spices used in Indian cooking.

visitors are free to explore the dynamic cuisine and culture of India in all of its flavorful glory.

Everything is vegetarian, but on Wednesdays and Sundays, Govinda's buffet is completely vegan. Food choices range from sweet to spicy, with curries, tofu, and selections of rice and naan. The lunch buffet is very reasonable, and diverse enough that diners could eat lunch there on a Tuesday and return on a Thursday to find a completely new lineup of food. Dinner is slightly more expensive, of course, but for an endless gourmet buffet of delectable and exotic food, it's still hard to beat.

It's still wonderfully accessible to those poor souls incapable of coping with spicy foods. Additionally, there's a full salad bar section for roughage and homemade dressings, too.

Cap it off with a mean mango lassi, a perfect sweet treat.

Hare Krishna Temple and Cultural Center
1320 West 34th Street
Houston, TX 77018
832-831-9951, govindashou.com

HUGS AND DONUTS

Food fads are a fickle beast. The ebb and flow of culinary popularity creates cyclical patterns of interest.

Brussels sprouts, for example, were long derided for their stinky, soggy existence until they suddenly appeared on every chef's menu.

Cronuts are perhaps the best—and most recent—example of a trend enjoying waves of cultural recognition, spreading from New York, where customers clamored to sample flaky treats created by pastry wizard Dominique Ansel. The cronut primarily owes such sudden fame to the familiarity of its two culinary forebears: donuts and croissants.

Whereas Frenchmen likely reach for flaky, crusty croissants at breakfast, Houstonians are far more likely to reach for donuts or kolaches. Thankfully, locals in need of circular sweet treats have plentiful options, few more comforting and consistently delicious than Hugs and Donuts.

Co-owners Jason Hill and Matt Opaleski originally rose to prominence in town with their now-retired food truck, H-Town strEATs. Not wanting to involve private investors, the duo turned to a more modern, 21st-century fundraising format for the donut shop: Kickstarter.

Their crowdfunding efforts paid off, raising almost $60,000 by offering incentivized investment packages for backers. "Black cards" were available for $50, entitling the holder to one free donut daily for twenty years. Buy-ins of $350 dollars included a hand-carved inscription of the backer's name on the wooden chairs dotting the diminutive dining room.

Simpsons-inspired menu staple "The Homer," topped with homemade strawberry frosting and sugar sprinkles, exemplifies Hugs and Donuts's playful appeal. Fresh fruit, matcha, or Boston cream can be found in the filled donuts. Fruity Pebbles atop sweet-and-

Left: The Pimp C, named after one half of the legendary Port Arthur rap duo UGK. Bun B, the surviving second member, is basically Houston royalty.

Middle: Fruity cereal bits on a sweet cream frosting atop a perfectly crunchy and effortlessly dense cake donut.

Right: Bunch of donuts. One could presumably bring enough for the entire office. Or, one could eat every single donut on the drive in and not tell a soul.

tangy frosting and salted caramel cake donuts similarly stand out. Even gluten-free options like the fan-favorite Oreo donut take turns on the always fresh, ever changing daily menu selections.

Kolaches, an Eastern European pastry introduced by Czech immigrants in the rough-and-tumble early days of Texas are given a similarly whimsical twist. Fillings like spicy jalapeño-cheddar sausage or smoked barbecue brisket from some of the city's best brisket masters are wrapped in bread and baked, providing savory counterparts for diners lacking a sweet tooth.

A donut without coffee, however, is like dancing with no music. Espresso drinks and coffee provide perfect counter notes to the dulcet donuts. Cold-brewed coffee is on tap alongside chocolate and strawberry flavored milks for kids—and kids at heart.

And the hugs? Those are totally free. Just ring the bell on the front counter.

1901 North Shepherd Drive
Houston, TX 77008
713-485-6443, hugsanddonuts.com

THE BREAKFAST KLUB

The Breakfast Klub is special. In Midtown Houston, the Breakfast Klub has served hearty home cooking since its opening in 2001. On any given morning, representatives from nearly every rung of society wait in line to experience the Breakfast Klub cuisine. Sometimes they wait for a very long time.

Owner Marcus Davis personifies the entrepreneurial spirit. Recognizing a dearth of soul-food breakfast restaurants around town, Mr. Davis, a Houston native, saw opportunity. Breakfast should be memorable, not methodical. The Breakfast Klub wings and waffles are certainly memorable.

It's some of the best fried chicken to be had, pairing salty crunch with a sweet waffle served with strawberries and dusted with powdered sugar. If the sweet and savory doesn't appeal, try their catfish and grits. Everything is big and bold, from the huge coffee mugs to their eggs Benedict, with giant slabs of ham, turkey, and bacon.

The Breakfast Klub has burgeoned into one of the city's most

"It caters to the culture," says celebrated local author and Breakfast Klub fan Van G. Garrett. "People wait in crazy lines for it, just to possibly meet someone influential. It's diverse. To see people who might not have conversations having conversations; it's a true metaphor of how food brings people together. It's a cultural phenomenon. Every time I pass by, I hope I get a red light just so I can have an opportunity to see who is in line. People go to see and be seen. Certain days, you can pass by there and it is like a club. Just waiting to get in."

That's what's up.

Top: A mural of President Barack Obama, one of the many works of art both inside and outside of the Breakfast Klub.

Left: Look for the yellow paint job and long lines.

Right: The famous chicken and waffles. Photo by Jayme Caturbani Bottom.

beloved eateries. National recognition duly followed, as did the patronage of luminaries like Beyoncé and a smattering of politicians and famous athletes. Bun B might show up, or maybe the Mayor. There might be cameras shooting segments for TV shows or local news. Steve Harvey gave them an award.

Open for breakfast and lunch seven days a week, the Breakfast Klub also has late night hours on Fridays and Saturdays from 10 p.m. to 3 a.m.

Final warning: waits can be long, but the staff, service, and amazing food make up for it.

3711 Travis Street
Houston, TX 77002
713-528-8561, thebreakfastklub.com

SARAH PLACE

Xiao long bao are a Shanghai cuisine specialty. Commonly known as soup dumplings, these pockets of meat filling and soup should be contained by almost dangerously thin wrappings. The dough wrapping should hold together just enough for dumplings to be carefully transferred to a soup spoon without tearing. Soup dumplings are incredibly time-consuming to prepare, but the end result is truly special.

Broth for the xiao long bao is made with pork and chicken parts, simmered in water alongside aromatics like ginger, garlic, and green onions, China's version of a classic French mirepoix. Gelatin is added at the end, allowing the broth to solidify into a more jelly-like consistency as it cools. Packed with all those beautiful flavors, the gelatin cubes get mixed with ground pork and usually shrimp, more aromatics, salt, and white pepper (not black pepper, though, which is far less common in Chinese cooking).

When the whole dumpling is put into a wooden bamboo steamer and cooked, the steam produces a phase change, melting the solid gelatin back into a liquid. A small bite should be taken from the skin once it's in the spoon, allowing some broth to seep out, releasing the sensuous, glorious soup.

Sip a little from the spoon, at first. Good soup dumplings are discerned by the wrapping, first and foremost. Ideally, the dough should be able to contain both liquid and filling, yet should never be so thick as to be gummy or tough. After trying some of the soup, top it with some chili oil or black vinegar.

Fair warning: make sure to blow on the filling and also allow the piping-hot steam to escape first before biting in. Burning the top of your mouth on overly microwaved pizza isn't remotely in the same ballpark as biting into hot soup dumplings. They will snatch the soul right out of your body.

Top Left: It's in a busy parking lot. Luckily, there's a sign.

Top Right: Congealed fat mixed with chili oil from the soup dumplings.

Bottom Left: Har gao. Shrimp dumplings with massive chunks of chopped shrimp.

Bottom Right: Xiaolongbao. Shanghai Soup Dumplings. Served with a dipping sauce of ginger steeped in black vinegar.

Houston's Chinatown is the kind of place where, with proper motivation, just about anything can be found. Other places serve soup dumplings, too, but often have a more difficult threshold for entry, whether it's language barrier, confusing location, or overly picky dining companions.

Muted interiors and varied selections of regional Chinese dishes make Sarah Place stand out. Sarah Place's har gao are perfectly steamed shrimp dumplings made more perfect by some chili oil. Meals are best when shared with family and friends at Sarah Place, but service is always friendly and accommodating.

9968 Bellaire Boulevard, #160
Houston, TX 77036
713-995-0985

DOLCE VITA

Marco Wiles brought a modern taste of Northern Italian cuisine to Houston when he opened his upscale namesake Da Marco in 2000.

Each year, Chef Wiles presents a white truffle dinner featuring several courses incorporating truffles from Piemonte, Italy, paired with wines from the same region. Tickets for the 2018 meal were $375 a person. Reservations are required, and there is a dress code: elegant/business attire; no sneakers, shorts, sandals, sportswear, or baseball caps.

As the dress code suggests, they don't serve just anybody. Famously—according to a former *Houston Press* writer—Wiles's wife Gloria once supposedly turned down the Rolling Stones. The British rockers reportedly called late one Saturday for a table after a Houston concert. Da Marco's was simply too busy.

Gloria and Marco own two other popular Houston restaurants.

Da Marco is upscale elegance.

Vinoteca Poscol is meat and cheese, shared plates, and wine— perfect for happy hour or an amorous evening of drinks, finger foods, and candlelight in an intimate setting.

Somewhere in the middle is Dolce Vita, sort of like the littlest bear in "Goldilocks and the Three Bears." The porridge isn't too hot, and everything else is just right.

Dolce Vita is knowns for excellent pizza, served uncut on little metal risers with a large steak knife for dividing it up—as it would be served in Naples. The steak knife presupposes the question of whether pizza is to be consumed with either hands or silverware. It actually answers the question. All pizza must be cut at some point. At Dolce Vita, it's merely left up to customers. Cut it diagonally. Hell, cut it into stars and stripes. As American as the choice of how to cut a pizza is, this is very much how it would be served in Naples.

Top Left: Classic, simple pepperoni pizza from Dolce Vita (Italian for "sweet life").

Top Left: Sign at the narrow entrance off Westheimer.

Bottom Left: Margherita; buffalo mozzarella, red sauce, and basil.

Bottom Right: Tallegio pizza, with gorgonzola, pears, arugula, and truffle oil.

Neapolitan pizzas are cooked so hot and fast the center must rest after coming out of the oven. Like a piece of meat, the juices will all run off, and the ambient heat won't finish cooking the very center.

Expect the center to be a little runny. Although it's not what corporate delivery chains serve, Naples is where pizza was invented.

Even ordering pizzas 'well done' only accounts to a few more seconds of the pie held in the top part of the oven. This technique, known as "doming," ensures pizzas are a little more well done toward the middle.

It's fantastic either way.

500 Westheimer Road
Houston, TX 77006
713-520-8222, dolcevitahouston.com

Menus and restaurants continually evolve. Some changes, like menus featuring brussels sprouts or emphasizing sustainable meat and produce sourcing, work well. Other trends aren't so lasting or worthwhile, like needlessly confusing fusion concepts, or endless parades of Poke shops opening, serving such abominations as sushi burritos stuffed with imitation crab and sriracha mayo.

Recently, it seems people have been starting to pay more attention to where their food comes from and what's in it. Restaurants have rightfully responded to this demand for transparency, making efforts to provide customers with healthy, local, ethically sourced options. Even corporate chains and fast food restaurants are making some efforts toward catering to this shift in public demand.

This trend reflects a growing awareness by consumers. Current projections have close to a third of the country's population considered obese. By 2030, the number of obese adults in America could potentially reach as high as 50%. This is a serious problem. The more awareness and action from industry and consumer alike predicates a necessary change.

Benjy Levit and Dylan Murray inherently understood this need. Successful, respected business partners in the restaurant industry, the duo's 2011 Local Foods debut location in Rice Village forced people to pay attention. National and local media were aware, at least.

The "Crunchy" Chicken Sandwich at Local Foods is absolutely worthy of the praise, recognized as one of the country's best meals between sliced bread. Layers of crunchy textures surround cold, pulled chicken, topped with pickles and a dill-heavy ranch dressing. Roasted nut crumbles and smashed house made potato chips give a roasty-toasty crunch, salty and a bit sweet between the whole wheat bun and some shredded lettuce.

Left: Outside patio. In Houston this is an option about four months out of the year. It is too hot otherwise.

Top Right: 420, bro. Downtown location.

Bottom Right: Yes, please. According to most doctors, watermelon sangria can actually take the place of water in your daily diet. This is a fact. Don't bother looking it up.

Now, five locations around Houston are serving up healthy, delicious salads and sandwiches to ample lunch crowds. Nightly dinner specials complement their beer, wine, and cocktails, along with other enticing menu options, with each location offering a slightly different twist on a similar theme.

The downtown location has some fresh seafood options and a raw bar in addition to a signature burger. A free-range, grass-fed beef patty from 44 Farms, a supplier for many of the city's best restaurants, is a decadent alternative to the otherwise organic roughage.

Nightly dinner specials like chimichurri roast chicken, gulf shrimp, and crab gumbo can smooth over the wrinkles of a long day in the office. Vegan chicken fried mushroom steaks and chili corn chip pies do the trick, too.

Multiple Locations

713-255-4440 (Upper Kirby Location), houstonlocalfoods.com

TIGER DEN NOODLE HOUSE

Mike Tran really just seems to love opening restaurants in Houston. His first, Aka Sushi House, has long been a hip and popular sushi restaurant with one of the city's best Happy Hours. By 2019, Tran will be operating no fewer than nine other places around town, with a high concentration of his establishments located in Chinatown's massive shopping centers off Bellaire.

Tiger Den, his homage to traditional Japanese ramen, opened in 2013 to rave reviews and long lines.

Neither the raves nor lines have abated in the ensuing years. Hand-pulled noodles and a twenty-four hour broth process makes Tiger Den's ramen rich, flavorful, and well worth the wait.

Houston has by no means escaped the ramen craze of the last few years. Ramen shops have been popping up around town for a while, now. Tran proved prescient by getting skin in the game so early. Franchises all over the country have opened up new locations in Houston, cluttering the ramen marketplace.

Yet, the busy sign-up board outside Tiger Den is always full, and even on hot summer nights people will wait in line for the hot, simmered soup. There is more than just ramen, too. Izakaya-style small plates like yakitori and edamame are also served. Though the menu focuses on Japanese classics, there are still wonderful surprises. There are delectably fried, sweet and puffy pandan donuts and even tsukkamen, a deconstructed ramen with condensed, intense broth served alongside undressed noodles to dip, slurp, and savor the wonderful flavors.

Dun Huang Plaza
9889 Bellaire Boulevard, Suite D-230
Houston, TX 77036
832-804-7755, tigerdenhtx.com

TIGER DEN

饭堂

Ishin Udon is Tiger Den's counterpoint in Tran's restaurant group, serving traditional and elevated udon bowls for fans of a thicker noodle.

Top: Tonkatsu ramen.

Left: Yakitori skewers. There's a whole range of meat and veggie options.

Right: Storefront. The next-door neighbor, Laki Fish, is a poke spot from the same owner.

HICKORY HOLLOW

Fried chicken forever remains the crown jewel of Southern cuisine. Immediately familiar yet pleasantly refined, platters of golden brown chicken pieces elicit contented sighs of pleasure from carnivorous folks.

In Texas, though, there exists a dish which is possibly even more treasured and iconic: chicken-fried steak.

A bastardized amalgam of multiple cultures, chicken-fried steak is a Lone Star staple. It's certainly confusing to visitors, as the dish is not actually chicken. Tough beef steaks are pounded thin and fried, much like Wiener schnitzel. In fact, the Austrian and German immigrants settling in Texas starting back in the 19th century are considered the dish's originators. Its importance to Southern cooking, however, is not up for debate.

When factoring quality, history, and sheer quantity, few places manage to scratch the CFS itch quite like Hickory Hollow. Owner Tony Riedel bought the original location in Northwest Houston from a married couple in 1979. Recipes for the now-famous chicken-fried steak and Texas River Bottom gravy, generously served alongside in bowls, were delivered part and parcel in the purchase.

Chicken-fried steak is not like Texas barbecue. Sauce may be optional for ribs, but much of what makes a good CFS is the gravy, and Hickory Hollow's creamy, peppery variety is a perfect partner for the crunchy breading and dense meat.

Riedel stayed true to the founder's roots. Successfully serving his customers authentic country cooking allowed an expansion to a Heights location in 1987. The second location along Washington sadly closed in 2018, but the original remains authentically Southern. Stepping into Hickory Hollow is like stepping backward into a time when kitsch was king and wood paneling was queen.

Chicken Fried Steaks

Featured on the Food Network

With "made from scratch" Texas River Bottom Gravy

Served with 2 Side Orders

sub Baked Potato for 1 Side +2.49

Large **Rancher** – the "Saddle Blanket"	14.99
Medium **Hired Hand** – "Texas Size"	12.99
Small **Plowman** – "Perfect for lunch"	10.49

Top Left: What else does one need in life?

Top Right: The sizes and prices for your CFS experience.

Bottom left: The Small Ploughman. Really, there's nothing small about it.

Bottom Right: Large Rancher, pre-gravy soaking.

A loyal and long-standing clientele of older folks, families, and blue collar–types still fill the seats at the original Fallbrook location, and Hickory Hollow continues to thrive serving rib-sticking selections like barbecue and fried catfish in heaping portions.

However, the chicken-fried steak here is famous for good reason.

The Large Rancher, a gigantically delicious twenty-two ounces, has been on Food Network and Travel Channel shows featuring outrageous food challenges. Diners watching their figures can instead order smaller versions of the dish, like the Small Ploughman or the Medium Hired Hand. For sides, definitely give some consideration to the green beans and mashed potatoes. Or, sample the famous hot tots. The fried globes of mashed potato and jalapeño are reminiscent of a redneck arancini.

8038 Fallbrook Drive

Houston, TX, 77064

281-469-52323, hickoryhollowrestaurant.com

On Houston's south side, a sizeable Indian/Pakistani community brings a variety of ethnic flavors and flair. On Harwin Street, just about every kind of knock-off handbag is sold, and there are numerous tea, spice, and small grocery stores with rare treats from afar not easily found.

There are also many great places to eat.

Located off the Southwest Freeway at Hillcroft, Himalaya Restaurant & Catering is an unassuming strip mall eatery that happens to be one of Houston's most celebrated spots. Television shows and celebrity chefs have visited Himalaya over the years, adding on to this Indian-Pakistani restaurant's fame.

Chef Kaiser Lashkari has deftly fused numerous cuisines on his menu, from Tex Mex to Southern, Indian, and even Cajun. Using Southern techniques and flavors, he serves weekend specials like smoked brisket and even a spin on étouffée with crawfish and spicy masala gravy. Served alongside more standard, regional dishes like tikka masala and all manner of kabobs, the menu is replete with ample vegetarian options and an expansive list of sweet treats for dessert. Himalaya's lunch specials are the easiest way to experience some of what they do so well. Served on a lunchroom cafeteria tray, diners get a sizeable combination of curries, rice, vegetables, and naan for under $15.

It's BYOB! Definitely bring some beer or wine to help cool the spicy curry dishes. Also, right next door is the Colorado Club, one of Houston's most popular gentlemen's establishments. If the curries aren't hot enough, perhaps something of a more prurient nature will get the blood pumping.

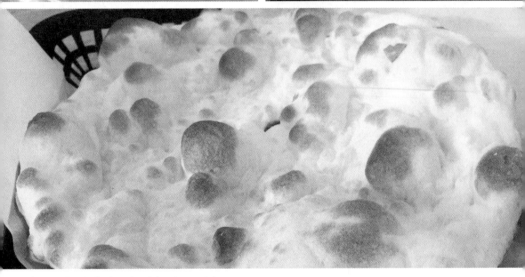

Top Left: Himalaya's lunch special.

Top Right: Storefront. In industry terms, that means "the front of the store." I know; it's complicated.

Bottom: Naan must certainly rank among the world's great breads: crispy yet pliable enough to fold and scoop up rice and curry.

Chef Lashkari has strict rules that his dining room customers must follow, particularly about things like dividing checks, BYOB requirements, and order limitations when the restaurant is busy. Regardless, the excellent food and media attention ensure Himalaya's continued acclaim.

6652 Southwest Freeway
Houston, TX 77074
713-532-2837, himalayarestauranthouston.com

DON CAFÉ & SANDWICH

I was flooded with recommendations when beginning this book. Out of all the unsolicited advice, one place was consistently being mentioned: Don Café.

"You gotta' go down to Don Café" was said to me probably six times within the first few weeks of initial research. Some people didn't even know the name or got the name wrong entirely. Always, though, the advice was the same: "Get you a banh mi from that Don place."

Don Café is a tiny, hole-in-the-wall Vietnamese deli where the most expensive menu item is less than $8. Each banh mi is served on warm, fresh baguettes stuffed with roasted meats and topped crunchy veggies like jalapeños and shredded carrots. When the rush is on and the employees are well and truly in the weeds, it's a marvel to watch the culinary engineering that transpires behind the cramped counter at Don.

Sandwiches are slapped together like clockwork, and it is not uncommon to see customers walking out with a bag of twenty sandwiches. In fact, it's an excellent and thrifty way to feed a whole office. Colleagues will be impressed by the gesture, but also by such impressive knowledge of Houston's ethnic food scene.

Don's banh mi are inexpensive so it won't break the bank, but be aware that Don Café is cash only; they do not accept credit cards.

There is a bounty of such establishments in Houston's Chinatown. Cheap, delicious home cooking is almost priceless. However, paying $5 for it isn't too bad, either.

9300 Bellaire Boulevard
Houston, TX 77036
713-777-9500

Left: Don Café front sign. A lot of the Chinatown strip mall spots can be hard to find, so the identifiable location is a nice touch.

Top Right: Banh mi, papaya salad, two orders of spring rolls: Affordable and delicious.

Bottom Right: Barbecue pork banh mi, dressed with sriracha.

KATA ROBATA

When Chef Manabu Horiuchi opened Kata Robata in 2009 he found almost instant success and acclaim.

Somehow, it has only improved. Look no further than *Houston Chronicle* food writer Alison Cook, a two-time James Beard Awarded culinary critic. Cook releases an annual Top 100 Restaurant List for Houston. In 2016, Kata Robata ranked 11th. By 2017, they were 5th. Impeccable service, comfortable atmosphere, and inspired food reflect a culture of perfection at this Upper Kirby standout.

Awards, loyal fans, and critical acclaim from local and national outlets ensures Kata Robata continually ranks among the city's best sushi spots, but also as a top venue for dining out regardless of cuisine or location.

Hori, as he is affectionately known, wanted to cook from the tender age of ten. Graduating with honors from Japan's Tsuji Culinary Institute, Hori-san's career took him first to acclaimed sushi restaurants in Tokyo, where he expanded his expertise. Eventually, Chef Horiuchi was asked to serve as executive chef for Japan's Consulate General in Houston, cooking for diplomats and big shots, like James Baker III and Clyde "The Glide" Drexler.

Word spread, and when local restaurant group Azuma was hunting for a chef to helm their Japanese-inspired tapas restaurant, they didn't need to look much further. With foundations firmly rooted in tradition, Chef Hori borrows gladly from local ingredients and classical French techniques, like his foie gras and scallop sushi.

Three words: foie gras nigiri. It's one of their specialties, and a masterclass in decadence.

Left: King crab spoon with cold dashi and uni.

Middle: Lunch bento box. Affordable and incredible quality for the price.

Right: Texas Kobe beef skewers, sous vide for seventy-two hours.

Perfectly torched and seasoned foie slivers are layered over plump scallops and wrapped in thin strips of nori, decadent examples of technique and execution. Flown in regularly, selections of Tsukiji fish vary with availability. Certain menu standouts like Texas Kobe skewers and lobster mac and cheese are permanent, but Chef Hori rotates new, fresh menu selections regularly.

Known for pristine, cold waterways, Hokkaido produces some of the finest shellfish in Japan. Chef Hori's menu celebrates Japan's northernmost prefecture, serving Hokkaido scallops and uni. The uni has a creamy, seafoam texture; the scallops are fresh and perfectly sweet. Familiar items are available for the less adventurous, yet the artful, immaculately prepared food should be appreciated for the artwork it is.

Many of Houston's most talented chefs cut their teeth in Kata Robata's kitchen, learning the ropes from a master. For the truest experience, reserve an omakase seating at the sushi bar.

Omakase means "I'll leave it up to you." Put your trust in Hori-san's talented hands. They won't disappoint.

3600 Kirby Drive
Houston, TX 77098
713-526-8858, katarobata.com

HUBCAP GRILL

A really great hamburger is a special thing. Many purists will argue a traditional arrangement of ingredients should somewhat align with a proper Chicago hot dog, i.e., fresh salad stuff and mustard.

Others align with a school of thought favoring mayo as the preferred condiment. Some stick to plain meat and cheese basics, yet there's always that segment of the dining community that wants outlandish additions like bacon jam, fried onion strings, parmesan crisps, or wasabi mayo.

All of these iterations are as correct as they are incorrect. Like most things, it comes down to perspective. Ketchup is fine on a burger, as far as I am concerned, but the very idea of putting sugar-sweet tomato paste onto a burger would be revolting to a lot of people. Similarly, this may apply to exotic meats, barbecue sauce, or green chilies.

Anyone accustomed to regional, distinct burger profiles—places like White Castle, Whataburger, In-N-Out, or practically any East Coast diner worthy of mention—would have an outright conniption at the idea of Philly cheesesteak burgers and Greek burgers.

Thankfully, owner and founder Ricky Craig couldn't give one ounce of a hot damn about what anyone thinks. Turkey or veggie patties won't be found on his menu. The beefy grind here has ample fat-to-meat ratio. Biting into one of Craig's craggy patties produces a luxurious sensation, with a deep flavor and plenty of fatty drippings to coat the face and hands. Light, proprietary buns provide chewy bounce to every burger, ensuring even the most basic offering is much more complex than its individual parts.

Many people simply laugh it's so good. It's purely mystifying, the type of meal that silences even the chattiest of tablemates. All they can do is shrug, shake their heads, and somehow chuckle while frowning.

With an inauspicious start, Ricky Craig's epicurean empire grew out of serving burgers from both a food truck and his original stand-alone

Left: Hubcap's famous Philly cheeseburger.

Top Right: Outside view of the original location on Prairie Street in Downtown Houston.

Bottom Right: They even have their own line of sodas.

shop, a slender Downtown location on Prairie Street. Still only open from 11 a.m. to 3 p.m., the Prairie location can fit a mere handful of people. Yet, it was so popular and so well liked, *Texas Monthly* magazine ranked Hubcap's decadent Philly cheesesteak burger number five overall in its 2016 listing of Texas's Top 50 Burgers.

With success comes criticism, and Hubcap has faced its fair share. Yet, meanwhile, their expansion to multiple locations all over town speaks for itself.

Really, it's only just a burger after all.

1111 Prairie Street
Houston, TX 77002
713-223-5885, hubcapgrill.com

HOUSTON LIVESTOCK SHOW AND RODEO

Anyone planning on visiting Houston should ensure their trip falls during this yearly event. 'Event' is actually too pitiful a word for describing this almost month-long celebration of all things Texas.

Rodeo events like bull riding, barrel racing, and calf roping occur each night followed by live music. Concerts feature acts that mainly cater to country music fans. Pop stars and rock acts are also featured, but the largest attendance each year is usually Go Tejano Night.

Mutton Busting alone makes attending the Rodeo portion of each night's festivities requisite. Young kids are put into pads and ice hockey–style helmets and plopped unceremoniously onto the backs of wary, frightened sheep. With little else to cling to but curls of wool, the kids hang on for all their worth. The sheep are given a firm slap on their hind quarters, and they take off like a bat out of hell.

More often than not, the kids only last a few seconds before they're tossed off like a sack of potatoes, but occasionally one makes it the entire way through the narrow course. This always elicits a raucous cheer from the appreciative crowd. Who doesn't enjoy a little child endangerment, after all? Well, some of the participants' tears

The Houston Livestock Show and Rodeo contributes a massive amount of money to the local economy, with one estimate equating it to Houston hosting a Super Bowl every year. It is also philanthropic by nature, raising millions every year in college scholarships for high school students participating in the Livestock show. 2017 was a record year for the event, raising almost $30 million in scholarships and grants. Well over two million people attended.

Left: A whole suckling pig, roasting away in front of the Houston First tent during Cook Off.
Right: Carnival and fair grounds. All kinds of food are available on a stick, including fried butter.

somewhat answer that question, but for the most part kids love it.

For the millions in attendance each year, though, the Livestock Show and Rodeo is about something else entirely: food. At the outdoor Carnival, between the rides and games, are more fried fairground foods than one can shake a stick at. In fact, many are on sticks, like fried butter, fried shrimp, or spiral-cut whole potatoes. If it can be fried, it will be, like some sort of fried Field of Dreams. If you fry it, they will come. When they come, they will eat.

Cookoff, the local term for the World Championship Bar-B-Que Contest that helps kick things off every year, is an event worth spending all day and night at. Teams come from all over to compete, and while many are private tents, there are plentiful opportunities for free food and drink after the cost of admission. There is even a wine event and auction for the more refined palates, offering varietals from all over the globe to sample and bid on.

It's big, loud, and terribly fattening. It's also a whole hell of a lot of fun.

NRG Parkway
Houston, TX 77054
832-667-1000, rodeohouston.com

BARNABY'S CAFE

Humans do not deserve dogs. Not at all.

We are their entire life while they occupy only a painfully small part of ours.

Sometimes, though, we get a chance to do something more for our four-legged friends than mere belly rubs or the unwanted end of a half-eaten pizza crust. This is exactly what Jeff Gale wanted to show when he opened the original Baby Barnaby's with his business partners in 1992. Today, his tribute to our furry friends has outposts all over Houston.

Barnaby was Gale's childhood English sheepdog. He was a very good boy. He was such a good boy that many years later, when Jeff Gale opened the original Baby Barnaby's with his business partners in 1992, he honored the memory of the shaggy, beloved English sheepdog of his childhood by naming the restaurant after him. Every one of Barnaby's multiple locations have murals depicting his adventures.

Baby Barnaby's on Fairview Street is an institution, situated in the heart of Montrose. It serves breakfast until noon on weekdays and 2 p.m. on weekends. Parking can be a nightmare, but free coffee is available outside, easing the strain of weekend crowds. The interior is cramped, loud, and always packed while embracing the lively, rollicking crowds. Country breakfast foods like chicken-fried steak and home fries reward the patience of those who wait.

> In 1999, owner and founding partner Jeff Gale was asked by the Houston Press if there would be any more than the original three locations in operation at the time. "Oh, no, no, no. Definitely not," he said. Today there are eight locations, as well as three pizza places called Luna Pizza, named after one of the other three founding members.

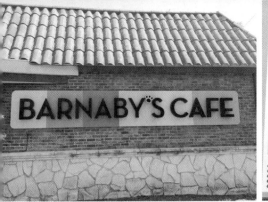

Left: Beautiful inside and out. If everyone cared for each other like the staff members at Barnaby's do for their guests, then the world would be a better place.

Right: Healthy, satisfying chicken, rice, and broccoli.

Lunch and dinner are served at Barnaby's other locations, but eating there any time reveals one of their keys to success: enormous portions. The food is healthy and well prepared, and pretty much any dietary need can be accommodated, as well—even the need to bring your very own furry best friend. The outdoor patios are always dog friendly.

A sizable section of the menu is devoted to a lineup of fantastic hamburgers for whenever a burger urge may strike. Classic bacon cheese burgers or turkey burgers topped with biting pesto and grated parmesan join a number of meatless patties all sure to satisfy. Barnaby's oversized salads are big enough for two, while meatloaf, chicken dishes, and appetizers like the dangerously addictive, Asian-inspired chicken wontons round out the menu.

Barnaby's many locations have been popular neighborhood cafés for many years. Service is brisk and friendly, if a bit brusque—busy servers buzz about like culinary versions of Johnny Cash in black t-shirts and jeans. The consistently high quality food comes out with fast, friendly service to all.

604 Fairview Street (Baby Barnaby's Location)
Houston, TX 77006
713-522-0106, barnabyscafe.com (directions and menus for all locations)

KOREAN NOODLE HOUSE

Korea is a beautiful country. I lived there for a year after college, working as a kindergarten teacher in Seoul. It was one of the best years of my life. I made friends from all over the world. Together we explored the beautiful strangeness that is life as a foreigner in large Asian cities like Seoul.

It can definitely be odd at times. Living abroad in a place where the language is different, and the people don't look the same is at once liberating and simultaneously terrifying. But it's always educational.

Eventually, the differences become less apparent. Over time, what becomes most obvious is how similar we actually are. Walking down the street becomes familiar, somehow. Seeing a mother scold her child—even though it's in another language—brings to mind a different mother.

A mom who would yell just like that, to do the dishes or clean up the dog crap in the back yard. And suddenly, without warning, some of the loneliness fades. Because as long as mothers are scolding children, the world continues to spin, and things are going to be OK.

Texas Monthly recently released a list of the world's best Texas-themed expat bars and eateries. Owned and operated by a group of Texas boys, Southside Parlor brings Southern soul to Seoul. Southside Parlor has become one of the city's most popular bars, successful enough to open a second, sustainable cocktail bar called Pocket. Robbie Nguyen and Phil Abowd, two of the founders, hail from Houston. They miss their families, of course, but they also miss the food. Robbie craves Viet-Cajun crawfish from HK Mart. Phil would give his right arm for Shipley's glazed donuts and a platter of sizzling fajitas from the Original Ninfa's on Navigation. Check them out if you're ever in Seoul.

Left: Close up shot of the bibimbap.
Right: Scratch made kimchi, Korea's ubiquitous side dish served with every meal.

It also doesn't hurt that Korean food is phenomenal.

Koreans love food. It's a foundational aspect of how the culture functions. Korea's adherence to Confucianism predicates entirely a precise code of conduct for societal mores, and the table is a great place to build relationships and mutual understanding.

On Long Point Road in Spring Branch there is a Little Korea Town. This area in northwest Houston has an astounding selection of authentic Korean restaurants. Korean Noodle House is just one of them, but it is one of the best.

One of the grand ironies that expats face is only realized once they return home: that cheap, subsidized health care goes away, for one. The cops are scary again, as well, because they are so heavily armed. Worst, what became familiar—so normal—is gone.

Korean Noodle House serves all the hits, like bulgogi, bibimbap, and tteokbokki. Their haemulpajeon, a sort of crepe-like pancake with seafood and veggies in the batter, can compete with any restaurant or café in Korea. Sundubu, which are spicy stews served in hot stone bowls, come out boiling hot and ready to scald the tongue of impatient diners. It's worth it, though.

Order plenty of soju, Korea's version of sake. It goes down easy, but that doesn't mean it is weak.

10016 Long Point Road
Houston, TX 77055
713-463-8870, koreannoodlehouse.wixsite.com

A remarkably interesting late-night Houston destination can be found at the original Chinatown Tan Tan. Hundreds of late-night spots exist around town, but Tan Tan is different—displaying Christmas lights in perpetuity and featuring a menu with over 200 items. Bustling, immensely diverse crowds maintain a hectic pace into the early morning hours on weekends, when Tan Tan stays lit until 3 a.m.

Opened in 1986, Tan Tan is best enjoyed with a group of preferably hungry friends, and preferably after some light-to-medium drinking has occurred. It's the kind of place where immediately after ordering, you will probably think "Oh. We definitely ordered way too much food."

It is very likely you won't be wrong. Even if some of that too-large order isn't consumed, Tan Tan's affordability makes this a minor issue. Plus, Chinese and Vietnamese dishes make perfect leftovers the next day. Family-style ordering is best. Portions are generous, and many of the larger tables have rotating lazy Susans for easy sharing. Everything is meant to be shared family style, anyway.

House special rice cakes are a can't-miss. Thinly sliced rice cakes are fried with egg and topped with dried turnips, green onions, and crispy fried onion bits. Orders of these salty and crunchy appetizers fly out the kitchen faster than seemingly possible. Texture, temperature, and flavor make this dish a great meal starter. Chargrilled rice and vermicelli platters, crispy or soft spring rolls, and passable pho round out the Vietnamese options, but the Chinese-inspired dishes are the safe bet.

Cornstarch and hot oil form the perfect crispy coating that Chinese-American dishes are so famous for. However, Tan Tan's food is far more reflective of the city's melting pot identity than any sort of traditional ethnic cuisine.

Left: Take-out gluttony. Get extra egg rolls. You know you want to.

Top Right: Neon beacon at the Westheimer location.

Middle Right: Top-notch General Tso's chicken.

Bottom Right: House special rice cake.

Fine dining it is not, to be sure. Tan Tan's essential charm lies in its balance, both on the plate and in the atmosphere. Service can be curt, and the decor is somewhat underwhelming, to be perfectly honest. None of this at all matters, though, as you'll be having way too much fun.

Tan Tan's Chinatown location in Bellaire is still eclectic and electric. There is a second location in the Westchase district that is more relaxed and family oriented, but it is still a worthy landing spot for eating and partying with friends.

Just go. Order too much food and too many beers. It is totally fine. This is Houston. We don't judge.

6816 Ranchester Drive
Houston, TX 77036
713-771-1268, tantanrestaurant.com

Chef and owner Paul Petronella is Houston restaurant royalty. By blood or marriage, Petronella is connected to just about every major player in the city's dining landscape. He grew up in restaurants, which is not at all metaphorical. His uncle Nash and cousin Briana operate D'Amico's, a popular fast-casual Italian concept open since 1996. Petronella spent his youth bathed in tomato sauce and garlic fumes from the kitchen, taking naps in the back office and pilfering from the garnish bar. His extended family owns and operates a veritable empire of Houston institutions, some of the oldest and most venerated restaurants in town. The service industry is ingrained in his genetics by this point.

The time spent in his uncle's restaurant was formative. After college, travels through Italy, and a brief cup of coffee in the corporate world, Paulie turned toward home and took over his parents' successful counter-service fast-casual spot, lovingly named after their dear son. When Petronella took over, he invested heavily in the restaurant's operating capabilities. He partnered with local coffee consiglieres Greenway Coffee to overhaul the coffee program, bought an industrial extruder to make all the pastas in house, and tweaked the menu and recipes to his liking.

Such concern and purpose can be seen each day in Paulie's. Affordable, scratch-made pasta dishes pair exceptionally well with crisp, gigantic salads and paninis. Standouts include the canestri alla funghi, with finely chopped garlic, shitake, and crimini mushrooms clinging harmoniously to rigid elbows of pasta in creamy marsala-sage sauce. Or, rich, pillowy meatballs and spaghetti finished in a delicate marinara are sure to cure the pangs of hunger. Paulie's shrimp BLT has become a legendary sandwich, and though it's no longer on the menu, one of the best chicken parmesans around can nonetheless be special ordered. Paulie's shortbread cookies, made

Top Left: Primavera aglio e olio, a garlic lover's delight

Top Right: Paulie's expansive menu. Nightly specials like shrimp po'boys and eggplant parmesan should not be missed.

Bottom Left: The cookies made famous by Paulie's mother.

Bottom Right: Paulie's spaghetti and meatballs: two light, melt-in-your-mouth meatballs atop springy, freshly made spaghetti and a simple, rustic marinara.

famous by his mother, are the perfect finish to the home-style faire. Better yet, beat the ghoulish heat of Houston's heavy summers with creamy gelato flavors like Nutella rocky road or fig and mascarpone.

Affable, informed staff provides the kind of service found more often in white-tablecloth, fine-dining establishments. Paulie's defies service industry standards in favor of compensation and benefits, ensuring employees are well cared for and content.. Hard-working kitchen staff pump out orders even when busy lunch crowd lines snake out the door. Over its twenty-year existence, Paulie's has become a neighborhood institution for good reason.

1834 Westheimer Road
Houston, TX 7706
713-807-7271, pauliesrestaurant.com

Belgium does a number of things very well, and Cafe Brussels brings that expertise to Houston.

Waffles come to mind first, of course. Belgian waffles are delicious. There is really no argument to be made against them. Sweet, crispy edges surround a light and fluffy center, never too dense or filling, waffles made Belgian-style are good as anywhere, even J.J.'s Diner.

Beer comes next. Belgian beer is some of the best in the world, if not the best. Belgian monks have been brewing beers in their abbeys since the 7th century. The monks got approval from the Catholic Church to brew and distribute beer for fundraising, so it's easy to see how they prospered. Even though it was likely unintended, it's significantly easier to convince people an invisible man lives in the sky watching everything we do if that individual has been drinking high alcohol content beers all day. Regardless, there is something about the combination of Belgian food and drink that is surprising, comforting, and tasty all at once.

After drinking all that beer, people need something to soak it up. Belgian bar food is a bit more elegant than what we usually do stateside. Gone are the potato skins and nachos, replaced by croquettes or escargots.

Maybe the best dish, certainly one of the signature dishes of the region, are moule frites, mussels steamed and topped with a variety of sauces and served with thick cut, twice-fried French fries.

Cafe Brussels does all of this and more. It's an authentic slice of Belgian culture, with comfortable seating and a beautiful wooden bar area. Casual and relaxed, the menu provides diners with a diverse menu of excellent dishes, and the beer selection is second to none. Sample all of the classic Belgian beers on tap, like Chimay and Kwak. For first timers, ordering a flight of beers to sample a little bit of everything is best. A similarly extensive bottled beer and wine list is available, but no hard alcohol is served.

Top Left: Lots of wooden furniture and soft lighting make the tap room warm and welcoming.

Top Right: Mussels steamed in white wine with onions, leeks, and celery. Make sure to order fries and some extra bread to soak up the broth.

Bottom Left: A flight of Belgian beers.

Bottom Right: The front entrance.

Food and beer lures diners back to Cafe Brussels time after time. It's like stepping off the streets of Houston and into a bar in Belgium. Tickets to Europe are expensive. Not everyone is lucky enough to casually hop across the pond. Although experiencing first hand the beauty and majesty of Europe is profound, it's not always practical.

Cafe Brussels is the next best thing.

1718 Houston Avenue
Houston, TX 77007
713-222-6996, cafebrusselshouston.com

BUBBA'S TEXAS BURGER SHACK

There is no place in Houston more perfectly named than Bubba's Texas Burger Shack.

The original guy who owned the place was named Bubba. They serve burgers. It's a shack.

Not much else needs saying, but the unassuming location hides a history as unique as its aesthetics.

In 1985, original owner Bubba Gilliam moved the shack—an old key store on Westheimer—to its current location underneath Westpark Tollway between the West Loop South and South Rice Avenue. Bubba enjoyed five years of success before loyal customer Richard Reed bought the place. Reed feared seeing his favorite burger place shut down due to construction and abandonment of the area as viable restaurant territory. It was a savvy move.

Richard Reed's daughters, Erin and Allison, manage operations at Bubba's. Despite changing ownership, Bubba's remains true to its roots with hearty food and roadside burger stand practicality. Bubba's specialty is the buffalo burger. Leaner, healthier, and with more unctuous flavor, buffalo meat gives customers a break from the normal beef burger. Bubba's signature spice blend accentuates the rich meat. There are beef patties available as well as buffalo hot dogs and splendid, smoky, spicy buffalo chili, a great addition to any cheeseburger or dog.

As the classic Saturday Night Live sketch goes: "No fries! Chips!" There is no room in the tiny kitchen for a fryer, so they offer bags of chips as a side. Soda and beer deepen the icehouse feel of the old, weathered wooden shack.

Sitting outside on Bubba's ramshackle deck, the seats thrum with vibrations. Almost directly overhead, traffic on Westpark Toll Road puts a little bounce in everyone's step, albeit involuntarily. If that still isn't enough action, order a side of Bubba's 59 house hot sauce. It has a habanero kick that will satisfy chili heads.

Top Left: It's a shack. The back wall separates patrons from the freeway.

Top Right: Three slices of peppered bacon, flattened and crisped on the griddle alongside the patties.

Bottom Left: Buffalo bacon cheeseburger, pierced with a patriotic toothpick. Buffalo meat has about one third as much saturated fat as beef, making it an excellent option for low-fat diets. Adding three slices of bacon and American cheese is not advised for such diets.

5230 Westpark Drive
Houston, TX 77056
713-661-1622, bubbastexasburgershack.com

BERNIE'S BURGER BUS (page 126)

GOMMON BOND (page 192)

HUGS AND DONUTS (page 50)

LOCAL FOODS (page 58)

THE ORIGINAL NINFA'S ON NAVIGATION (page 140)

THE PASTRY WAR (page 154)

HUGO'S (page 38)

GOMMON BOND (page 192)

THE RICE BOX (page 172)

SAINT ARNOLD BREWING COMPANY (page 142)

THEODORE REX (page 190)

YOKUSHI ROBATA (page 196)

ROOST (page 176)

THE PIT ROOM (page 166)

CHOCOLATE SPICE COOKIE $1.50

Sesame Cookie $1.50

sorted
an Cookies
Biscotti

GELAZZI (page 120)

Ever since the early aughts, Houston's craft beer scene has exploded. Beer-centric bars have been opening up left and right, it seems. Even restaurants known for their wine collections now have cicerones in addition to sommeliers. Cheap domestic beer will always have a place: tailgates, tubing, or backyard games of cornhole, for sure.

Consumers are inclined to reach for something a bit more complex these days, even though they don't want to work any harder to get it. Platypus Brewing seems to understand this dichotomy. At their brewery and taproom off Washington Avenue, they cater to the gourmand and glutton in equal measures. Their beers range from light and crisp to dark and heavy, with seasonal varietals regularly moved in and out of their tap lineup.

Brew master Kerry Emberton brings a decade of experience working in the craft beer industry. The ownership team includes natives and transplants, with backgrounds and experiences as diverse as their draft list. There are Aussies, a Sugar Land native, Houstonians, and a long list of other beer-loving founders.

It's a brewery started by homebrewers, and it shows. Platypus's outside patio has plenty of playsets and yard toys for kids, drinking

The non-theory of intelligent design is pretty quickly (and correctly) disproven upon examining the physiology of the platypus. Platypuses are mammals, but they lay eggs. They are venomous, as well. They have webbed feet and duck-shaped bills, and even though they primarily live and hunt in and around the water, they close their eyes, ears, and noses while diving for prey. Also, they sleep up to seventeen hours a day, which is possibly the only thing about the species that makes any actual sense.

Top Left: Young gentleman Mayer Platt enjoys his sweet potato fries. He also enjoys slow crawls on the beach, staring idly at the world around him, eating, and grunting.

Top Right: A big, beefy burger with all the fixings.

Bottom Left: Flash fried brussels sprouts.

Bottom Right: A flight of Platypus beers. Don't let a dingo eat your baby, mate.

bowls for canine companions, and comfortable seating with lots of TVs for the grown-ups.

The food menu helps highlight many of the similarities between Texans and Aussies: meat, potatoes, and fried stuff. This is typical bar food, but done very well and with some surprises, including Australian favorites like meat pies and sausage rolls.

1902 Washington Avenue, Suite E
Houston, TX 77007
832-742-5003, platypusbrewing.com

CORKSCREW BBQ

"We don't just want to be a restaurant," says Nicole Buckman. "We want to be a destination."

A glance at the guestbook by the front door is evidence that this goal has been accomplished. People flock from all over the world for some of the best barbecue money can buy. This place is worth going out of the way for. Nicole, who co-owns Corkscrew BBQ with her husband Will, wants every visit to be an experience worth remembering. The lines are long, and it is a decent drive from Houston, but the food speaks for itself.

After one bite of fatty, succulent brisket, all the waiting and traffic—it melts away.

The Buckmans are adamantly committed to their craft. They don't really take vacations, for example. Will is head pit master. They both still wash dishes or cut meat as needed—there are no vacations because they work all the time. Despite awards and acclaim, though, what the Buckmans care most about are customers. They feel a responsibility to the hungry hordes of barbecue fans lining up each morning, sometimes hours before opening.

All of their energy goes into what they do, and much of it is spent ensuring everything served meets their exacting, precise standards. Customers who come late are often annoyed upon learning the meat is sold out, but the Buckmans certainly know what they are doing. They cook to capacity and not a single ounce over.

This isn't to be annoying. Rather, it makes certain everything they do is perfect.

Success has not slowed the husband and wife team since starting out of their house in 2010. Quickly outgrowing their kitchen, they upgraded to a series of successively larger trailers before securing a permanent location in 2015. All of this was accomplished without a single penny spent on advertising.

Top Left: Lean and fatty brisket, turkey sandwich, rib, mac and cheese. No sauce needed, fam.

Top Right: One of Will Buckman's many smokers.

Bottom Left: Lines form early. Missing out on brisket and ribs is a hefty price for showing up late.

Bottom Right: Get a number and be ready to wait. And do not leave the parking lot.

There was never a need.

Nicole Buckman has a fierce pride about what they do, and about her husband. She credits his work ethic as a key factor in what they do.

"It doesn't matter what he does. He will work his ass off. He could be a garbage man, and he'd be the best damn garbage man around," she says of Will.

When she's asked what it feels like to look out the window to see a hundred people waiting in the Texas heat for their food, she paused to take in the scene before answering.

"It's surreal," she says.

26608 Keith Street

Spring, TX 77373

831-592-1184, corkscrewbbq.com

Parents with young children have a difficult time dining out. If anything, it comes down to a paucity of choices. Kids are loud, messy, and distracting, making them terrible restaurant guests for everyone who is not their parents. Often, this reduces a parent's choice to chain restaurants, fast food, or hell holes with talking animatronic rodents and cardboard crust pizza.

At Little Matt's in West University, the doldrums of dining out with the whole family are supplanted with a friendly, fun environment for all. Kids can play in the arcade or bang away on the many iPads mounted along a wall. They can explore the candy shop or experiment with different combinations at the ICEE machines.

And it's all for a very good cause. Owner Jim Reid opened Little Matt's with a desire to help others in his position. So, he donates the restaurant's profits in a variety of ways to cancer patients and their families at Texas Children's Hospital, a leader in cancer treatment and research. Cancer is the second leading cause of death in America for children under the age of fifteen, with the average cost of treatment rising to as much as $500,000. Families, on average, pay close to $40,000 out of pocket in travel and expenses, an outrageous sum.

Reid's own son successfully beat two bouts of cancer at a young age. The experience inspired him to turn around and pay their good fortune forward. To date, Little Matt's has helped thousands upon thousands of families offset the staggering medical costs involved in treatment. If only we lived in a country where people didn't have to sell burgers and fries to treat pediatric cancer.

But that's just what Little Matt's is dedicated to doing. Serving standard American classics, and not leaning on pretense or high concept, the menu offers something for everyone. Yes, even the picky eaters, too. Chicken tenders, burgers, salads, and Southwest-inspired

Left: A big menu to please even the pickiest little eaters and plenty of women's magazines for the moms.

Top Middle: Need some sauce? They have every one ever made.

Top Right: Yeah, they have an Icee machine.

Bottom Right: Pretty straightforward. More signs. Everybody loves signs. Houston has the most signs, tremendous signs. Beautiful signs.

foods like taco bowls and burritos serve as the straightforward and approachable eating options.

Kids absolutely adore this place. It was designed with them in mind, but there is also enough for grown-ups to enjoy, like free adult beverages, for one, or the ability to give the kids a handful of quarters and have them buzz off for a few minutes of peace and quiet. Though a donation is suggested for the beverages, the peace of mind is free of charge.

6203 Edloe Street
Houston, TX 77005
713-592-6200

KILLEN'S BBQ

Ever had the kind of argument that doesn't stop replaying over and over in a permanent loop? The kind where a perfect comeback only occurs days later, after thinking about it a thousand times?

The French call this l'esprit d'escalier. Staircase wit. When our retort comes far too late, as we are metaphorically already halfway up the stairs, beaten and retreating. We owe the French many thanks for their cultural contributions: art, music, and food.

Not mimes, though. No, never mimes.

Houstonians owe a similar debt of gratitude to Chef Ronnie Killen. A graduate of Pearland High School, Chef Killen has stamped his influence on the culture of Houston's dining scene, and like that three-day-late insult, diners will find their thoughts drifting back continuously to Chef Killen's beef ribs in Pearland.

After graduating top of his class from London's Le Cordon Bleu, Chef Killen began his celebrated culinary career away from home. Killen returned to Houston in 2003, though, becoming executive chef at Brenner's Steakhouse. Under his guidance, Brenner's was named Houston's "Best Steakhouse" by the *Houston Press* and the *Business Journal*.

In 2005, Ronnie Killen was called about a new job, once again finding himself interviewing to be an executive chef, only this time at the White House. Killen had cooked for the Bush family on multiple occasions earlier in his career and was invited to Washington, D.C. for an audition. Killen was a finalist for the job, but ultimately lost out on the gig.

Never one to dawdle, Killen moved on. Now, his growing restaurant group has multiple concepts: Killen's Barbecue, Killen's TMX, Killen's Steakhouse, Killen's Burgers, and Killen's STQ, an updated, refined combination of both barbecue and steakhouse influences.

Left: Brisket, ribs, turkey, and smoked jalapeño and cheddar sausage. Not pictured: the beef rib. Photographs do not do Killen's beef rib justice. Only eating one does. Even still, this meat popsicle will likely cause eyes to widen and heart rates to elevate at first glance.

Right: Free cups! Free beer! Pay for the food, though. Photos by Sean Sloan.

Killen's Barbecue has satisfied customers since 2013. In addition to the gigantic, fork-tender beef ribs smoked on the hock, the menu features classic Texas barbecue staples like fatty brisket with peppery bark, smoked sausages, and an array of fantastic sides and desserts. Even the smoked turkey, so easy to dry out that most everybody does so, is done well.

Crowds outside Killen's Barbecue begin forming early, before doors even open. To accommodate the wait Texas-style, the staff drop kegs of Lone Star out on the front lawn in big trash cans covered with bags of ice, just like in college.

Everything moves quite quickly, as free beer and the smell of smoking meat in the air makes time fly by.

3613 East Broadway Street
Pearland, TX 77581
281-485-2272, killensbarbecue.com

MAINE-LY SANDWICHES

Lobster rolls weren't invented in Maine. Originally, the concept was developed in Connecticut.

This is by no means a ringing indictment of either state, nor of the lobster roll itself. Far from it. As far as perfect sandwiches go, lobster rolls possess a simplicity and charm surpassing the sum of their total parts.

Chilled chunks of sweet, boiled lobster are first mixed with just enough mayonnaise to bind them together. Combined with a dash of lemon juice, salt, and pepper, the concoction is stuffed into buoyantly pliable split-top buns. Griddled in butter, the warm, toasty buns provide ample purchase for the chilled lobster meat. All of the ingredients are subtle, making lobster the true star. Of course, the quality and freshness of the meat predicates a successful representation of the dish.

Which is the reason owner Melvin "Buddy" Charity flies lobsters in fresh from his home state of Maine each week. A former high school teacher, Charity originally ran the lobster rolls as a Friday-only special. However, fans clamored for more. There just isn't anything like it in town. His authentic slice of New England so lovingly served up continues to bring in the masses.

Fair warning, sailor: lobster rolls are the most expensive menu item. Deli-standard subs like ham, turkey, roast beef, or meatballs are available, dressed to order for an outstandingly affordable alternative.

Commodity is king, though. Maine classics like fried clam strips, lobster bisque, and chowder stand out in a city known for barbecue, burgers, and fajitas.

7620 Katy Fwy. #225
Houston, TX 77024
713-942-2150, mainelysandwiches.com

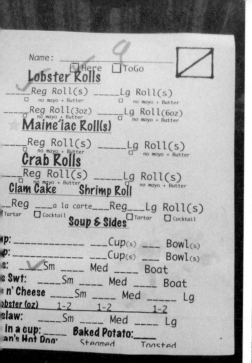

Name: ☑ Here ☐ ToGo

Lobster Rolls

_____Reg Roll(s)   _____Lg Roll(s)
  ☐ no mayo + Butter   ☐ no mayo + Butter

_____Reg Roll(3oz)   _____Lg Roll(6oz)
  ☐ no mayo + Butter   ☐ no mayo + Butter

Maine'iac Roll(s)

_____Reg Roll(s)   _____Lg Roll(s)
  ☐ no mayo + Butter   ☐ no mayo + Butter

Crab Rolls

_____Reg Roll(s)   _____Lg Roll(s)
  ☐ no mayo + Butter   ☐ no mayo + Butter

Clam Cake   Shrimp Roll

__Reg ___a la carte___Reg___Lg Roll(s)
☐ Tartar ☐ Cocktail   ☐ Tartar ☐ Cocktail

Soup & Sides

p: _____ ___Cup(s) ___ Bowl(s)
p: _____ ___Cup(s) ___ Bowl(s)
s: __✓_Sm ____ Med ____ Boat
s Swt: ____Sm ____ Med ____ Boat
n' Cheese ____Sm ____ Med _____ Lg
bster (oz)   1-2   1-2   1-2
slaw: ____Sm ____ Med ____ Lg
in a cup:____ **Baked Potato:**___
an's Hot Dog: Steamed   Toasted

Maine-ly SANDWICHES

NEW ENGLAND CLAM/LOBSTER SHACK
NO AIR FARE NEEDED!
GREAT MAINE DELIS TOO
ORDER ONLINE

Left: A simple, straightforward ordering system.

Top Right: The beautiful, luxurious lobster roll.

Bottom Right: Parking is around the back, and they aren't wrong that it beats flying to Maine.

ONE/FIFTH

To make even a single restaurant successful takes many months—if not years—of preparation, practice, and patience. Most new restaurants struggle, and many fail entirely.

Therefore, the idea of opening a new restaurant every September for five straight years would seem outrageous to many. Outrageous at the least. Impossible, even. At most, the idea of pulling the rug out from underneath customers every twelve months seems like bad business. Implementing an entirely different cuisine, menu, decor, and wait staff uniforms would absolutely boggle the mind of even the most seasoned service industry pro.

That's exactly what Chris Shepherd did, though. When a fine-dining establishment closed, Shepherd was offered a limited five-year lease on the property. Though it was located in one of Houston's most desirable locations, the restrictive time frame initially put him off. What did he have to prove? He was busy operating a thriving restaurant group already in the process of evolving.

It has become clear to his many fans that Chef Shepherd is nothing if not ambitious. Shepherd has a bounty of different ideas he could accomplish in five years. Those ideas turned into One/Fifth. Along with business partners Kevin Floyd and Whitney Mercilus, they decided to open an entirely different restaurant each year. For five years. New look, new concept, new everything.

It is a staggering undertaking but has succeeded beyond all expectations.

First came One/Fifth Steak, a call back to the classic steakhouses of old. That concept was so popular that Shepherd didn't want the steakhouse theme to end, so he did something even more radical. He closed his landmark Underbelly restaurant, an incredibly successful place, reopening it in fall of 2018 as a continuation of One/Fifth

Left: Beautiful design elements are showcased throughout One/Fifth.

Top Right: Old fashioned.

Bottom Right: Busy bar area churning out fantastic cocktails, with a beer and wine list matching each new concept.

Steak called Georgia James, the new iteration named in honor of Shepherd's parents.

Romance Languages came in Year Two, threading together the loosely interconnected strands of Latin, Spanish, and French cultures into a single knot. Year Three sees the team freshly operating as One/Fifth Mediterranean, taking diners on a ranging jaunt around the many overlapping segments of Middle Eastern cuisine.

Shepherd has accumulated an incredible amount of talent over the years. Their collective hard work and creativity are the only plausible explanation for the success of such a radical idea. One/Fifth's beverage team developed an outstanding wine list and a truly innovative cocktail menu, which augment the experience each time the restaurant boldly evolves.

1658 Westheimer Avenue
Houston, TX 77006
713-955-1024, onefifthhouston.com

HELEN IN THE HEIGHTS

It was Marlowe who wrote Helen's "... was the face that launch'd a thousand ships...."

Helen was supposedly daughter to Zeus. Married to King Menelaus of Sparta, Helen was considered the most beautiful woman anywhere in the world.

Helen of Troy meets Orlando Bloom (Paris of Troy). She runs off with him, and those thousand ships were launched from all across Greece to bring her back to Menelaus, her husband. Prince Paris gets Hector, his older (and way cooler) brother killed in the process, along with thousands more soldiers and civilians from Greece and Troy alike in the ensuing siege and invasion.

We all know what came after that.

The Greeks hid inside a big wooden horse, which was presented as a gift to the Trojans. Troy just opened up and let in the obviously harmless wooden horse. Once the sun set, the Greeks poured out and sacked the city.

It goes without saying that any restaurant referencing such stories understands the historical implications therein. Certainly, the place must be beautiful. Stunning, rather. It should be something worth remembering, worthy of praise and adoration. And Greek. It should be very Greek.

Helen Greek Food and Wine is just such a restaurant. Both locations are easily, certainly beautiful. And the food is certainly enough to launch those thousands ships.

The food is incredible. Varietals exclusively from Greece grace the extensive wine menu.

The wine list is as interesting a collection of wine as it is entertaining, with clever, witty descriptions of the various wines on offer. Verbatim, it reads:

"It's all Greek to me. This whole menu is Greek Wine. They might

Left: Cauliflower 'steaks' with roasted carrots and fresh herbs.

Top Right: Helen's Happy Hour is a great deal with half-off cocktails and affordable small bites.

Bottom Right: Helen's gyros are served like Greek Fajitas, on a sizzling platter with fresh pita.

give you mild panic attack. Have no fear. Every wine is available by the glass... you can ask [for] a taste of each wine and get buzzed for free (Please don't do that)."

Paris of Troy would consider that a challenge. Paired with Helen's fabulous dining options, the resulting meal will certainly leave diners full and happy. 'Build your own platters' of thinly sliced, roasted Black Hill pork gyros are great for sharing, and the plentiful veggie and appetizer options additionally make Helen a wise option for dining with groups. The interior of both the Heights and Rice Village locations are diminutive in size, but the bold flavors and eclectic wine collection more than make up for such a minor concession. Just don't steal anyone's spouse.

1111 Studewood, Suite B
Houston, TX 77008
832-582-7146, helengreek.com

CAMERATA

Wine bars can often be sort of intimidating. Servers and sommeliers drop terms in vernacular that average people likely aren't familiar with.

Most of us nod along, pretending to understand what the hell anyone means when referring to terroir, tertiary aromas, or lees. Most wine drinkers know their favorite varietal and whether it's red or white. Others know at least a few select terms like brut, corking fee, or bunghole, my personal favorite.

At Camerata, the staff carefully crafted an ambiance and environment that mostly avoids the more pretentious airs that often turn people off of wine bars. Some of the most vaunted industry stars in the city have spent time at Camerata. There is a culture of education and mentorship for employees, an openness and respect that in turn extends to customers.

They ask questions, and they listen. Recommendations are offered or withheld as needed, and there is no haughty sneer if you order the cheapest thing and sip it slowly. As long as customers are happy, so is Camerata's staff.

Paul Petronella owns Camerata, located next to his restaurant, Paulie's. The pair make a great combination for a pre- or post-dinner wine stop. Both places serve great food, but Paulie's is definitely more conducive to the sit-down meal experience. Meat and cheese are of course standard at most wine bars, and rightfully so. Camerata has amazingly well-sourced charcuterie, but the varied menu definitely bears further examination. Stellar dishes like foie gras mousse or marinated chickpeas with crostini are satisfying appetizers for pairing with the excellent wine selection. The carrots, however, are hauntingly good.

Left: Els Jelipins; it's a "unicorn" wine, handmade in Spain by a mother-daughter team. They only bottle a few thousand a year. If it's available, get it immediately.

Top Right: A full spread, with accoutrements like thyme honey, Marcona almonds, olives, house pickles, and bread.

Bottom Right: The carrots. Roasted, chilled, and topped with good stuff like basil pesto and shaved, frozen ricotta salata. Simply perfect and perfectly simple.

Roasted and served cold, rainbow carrots are dressed with pesto and sherry vinegar before ribbons of frozen ricotta are shaved over the top, forming a sort of salad. It's a dish hitting every note. Ask for a recommended wine pairing from Camerata's eclectic list—they are always happy to introduce guests to something new.

General Manager Chris Polodian was honored by Wine Enthusiast's "40 Under 40 Tastemakers" commendation in 2017, an award for influencers and up-and-comers within the wine industry. He was the youngest member of the award group at only twenty-seven and the only wine industry professional in the entire Southwest United States. Polodian hasn't changed much at Camerata's since taking over a few years back, keeping the environment approachable and relaxed. Camerata's clever menu descriptions, friendliness, and reasonable pricing make drinking wine elegantly simple.

1830 Westheimer Road
Houston, TX 77006
713-522-VINO, pauliesrestaurant.com/camerata

Stiff peaks and bright colors should be avoided. Gelato has much lower butter fat content than ice cream and should actually be covered to ensure the gelato is kept at proper temperature.

Whenever gelato vendors—particularly on the street or outside—have uncovered gelato standing at attention in angular, gravity-defying triangulation, this indicates the gelato is too cold, often masking artificial flavors. Bright colors are also likely to indicate the presence of food coloring.

Vendors serving blindingly fluorescent pistachio gelato are suspect. Pistachio gelato should be the same color as pistachios.

End of story. Same with something like grapefruit or strawberry: if they are an eye-assaulting, offensive color then give that vendor a wide berth.

The pistachio gelato at Gelazzi in the Heights represents the ideal of what this famous Italian confection should be. Creamy and not too overly sweet, Gelazzi gelato is riddled with little chunks of finely ground pistachio throughout, making this dessert a destination dish for lovers of the little green nut. My wife and I tried their pistachio gelato for the first time, purchasing a small cup we had planned to split during our drive home.

It was so good we turned around for another cup; the first one had been devoured.

With a wide selection of flavors and free samples, everyone can find a worthy confection to indulge in. If standard cups are too pedestrian, Gelazzi offers different waffle cones and affogato. Affogato is an espresso shot poured over gelato, an interesting confluence of temperature with texture.

Gelato is the Italian word for ice cream. Some of the grandeur and glamour surrounding gelato, particularly as an exotic counterpoint to standard ice cream, is somewhat blown out of proportion. However,

Left: Gelazzi lights up the night with the amazing pistachio gelato on a waffle cone.

Top Right: Neon beckons to Gelazzi guests on warm nights.

Bottom Right: Leave the gun. Take the cannoli.

the difference becomes apparent with the first taste. Gelazzi strives to be the best example of that difference anyone can find outside of Italy.

Everyone has that one family member who got a bit pompous after their first time traveling to Europe. These individuals enjoy pointing out the differences between cultures as if a two-week backpacking trip suddenly turned them into Rick Steves. Nowhere is this misplaced arrogance more prevalent than with food.

So the next time the snooty cousins come back from an Italian vacation, talking about dining al fresco with dark and handsome Italian men or how much better the food is in Italy, take them to Gelazzi.

Hopefully, it shuts them up for a while.

3601 White Oak Drive
Houston, TX 77007
713-597-6257, gelazzi.com

THE RICHMOND ARMS

British pubs have a long and storied history steeped in tradition and culture. However, they aren't really British.

Well, they are now. Shortened from "public houses," pubs now are distinctly British, assuredly. Pubs serve food and sell booze, but their role in British daily life is of vast importance. Long serving as gathering points for exchanging stories and news from near and far, some also function as inns, providing respite from the road for an evening.

But, again: they aren't really British. Not originally, anyhow.

The blueprint for pubs extends back 2,000 years, to the Roman invasion of the British Isles beginning in the year A.D. 43. In typical Roman fashion, a well-engineered system of towns and roadways was soon established, allowing Britannia to be traversed in new and novel ways. Travelers, of course, get thirsty.

Tabernae was the Latin term for the wine bars of antiquity, later to be called taverns as the English language evolved.

Soldiers need to stop, wash off the road, and quaff some wine. In fact, the oldest pub in England is located in Nottingham. Known as 'Ye Olde Trip to Jerusalem,' it served as pub and inn, a stop off for

On September 14, 1787, George Washington threw an epic party in a pub for the framers of our country and Constitution. Today, it would have cost almost $16,000, adjusting for inflation. More than forty-five gallons of booze were served to the fifty-five gentlemen in attendance. That does not include the extra twenty-one bottles of wine drank by the seven musicians who played the party. This is how our country was founded, by a bunch of dudes drinking gallons of booze and getting absolutely obliterated all while framing our great nation.

Left: The Arms's outside, English cottage-esque styling.

Middle Left: A true taproom. All the mugs hanging over the bar are for regulars.

Middle Right: The entire place is adorned with football (soccer) regalia.

Right: A proper pint of ale.

Crusaders joining in King Richard the Lionheart's many Holy Land conquests.

British folk were not as into wine as their continental cousins were. Beer and ale have always been reliable standards of the British diet. Partly, this was due to the intrinsic dangers of drinking water, but also because the British like getting drunk. At the time, ale was far safer to drink because most people knew diddly squat about sanitation. Some would argue they still don't, but what hasn't changed is the British taste for a pint or three.

The Richmond Arms holds true to convention. It's a place where football (soccer) fans can show up at seven in the morning for a full English breakfast plate and a pint of stout. A complete menu of classic pub fare like bangers and mash, shepherd's pie, and a hearty burger can ensure proper fuel for touring the eighty beers on tap or long matches of footy. Also, pub trivia nights are hosted every Wednesday, as infuriatingly difficult as they are entertaining.

Many places try to replicate an authentic British pub; more often than not, they fall well short. This is not so at the Richmond Arms. Grab a few pints and relax, mate.

It's quite lovely, innit?

5920 Richmond Avenue
Houston, TX 77057
731-784-7722

FRENCHY'S

New Orleans native Percy Creuzot didn't intend to become Houston's fried chicken empresario when he and his wife Sally opened their first restaurant on Scott Street. When they first opened, the husband and wife team sold the New Orleans–style po'boys that Percy grew up with. Everything changed when Jesse Hearns convinced the Creuzots to add fried chicken to the menu. Hearns, working at an adjacent car dealership, was certain it would grow business, allowing them to compete with the existing fast food chains close by.

Houstonians, he explained, had a learning curve with Cajun dishes, yet they understood fried chicken with no problem whatsoever. So, Hearns brought chicken into the kitchen to demonstrate how to season, bread, and fry it, techniques that earned Percy Creuzot the nickname now synonymous in Houston with fried chicken: "Frenchy."

Fortunes fared far better once the new menu item developed. Creuzot incorporated a fried chicken recipe acquired via family friends from Louisiana, tweaking it to perfection. Eventually, Creuzot developed the now-famous Frenchy's Fried Chicken Houstonians crave.

Business was slow to start. Though located just one block from University of Houston, Frenchy's made $14 dollars when doors

> Frenchy's son Percy III remembers his dad starting up the fryers and dropping in the chicken right after the local chains would close. Early on, they would stay open late, and Frenchy would be out in the street, flagging people down with a flashlight. He'd always take the money first; that way they wouldn't leave until they got their chicken. Late-night crowds make even men as kind and well-liked as Percy Creuzot cautious.

Left: Frenchy's dirty rice, one of their Cajun-influenced sides.

Middle: Sometimes the signs are blue; sometimes they are blue-green; this one is yellow.

Right: Close-up of a ten-piece order.

opened July 3, 1969. After adding Cajun-inspired fried chicken, however, the business blossomed, and hordes of hungry students returning to college for the fall semester came through.

Financial problems briefly derailed Frenchy's for a period of time in the 1980s. The original location remained in the family, with Creuzot's son retaining control. By the mid-2000s only three operating Frenchy's remained, but the family was undeterred and bounced back with new locations around the city. Percy Creuzot insisted on personally training cooks in new franchise locations.

In addition to the crispy, spicy chicken, Frenchy's serves plenty of dirty rice, buttery biscuits, mashed potatoes, and its famous lemon cake. Percy Creuzot passed away in 2010, but his innovative recipe for Cajun fried chicken has never changed, regardless of economics, shifting cityscape, or the cruel hand of chance. His interests certainly weren't limited to just chicken, however. Throughout his life, Creuzot was a loyal supporter of his community, giving graciously to the United Negro College Fund, Urban League, NAACP, and colleges like the University of Houston and Texas Southern.

Frenchy's can be summed up very simply: Beyoncé's favorite restaurant in her hometown of Houston is Frenchy's. After she came home to help locals recover from Hurricane Harvey's devastation, Beyoncé went to Frenchy's.

3919 Scott Street
Houston, TX 77004
713-748-2233, frenchyschicken.com

BERNIE'S BURGER BUS

Twenty-five percent of food trucks fail within their first year, while almost 60% close within the first three. Yet, somehow this burgeoning local chain defies those odds. Started from a modified yellow school bus with a fryer and grill, Bernie's now has multiple permanent locations, including those in Bellaire, the Heights, and Katy.

Chef and Owner Justin Turner came to town as a personal chef for former Houston Rocket Shane Battier after a 2006 trade from Memphis. In 2010, Battier was traded back to Memphis, but Turner chose to stay, laying down roots in Houston.

The success of Bernie's Burger Bus, named after Turner's grandfather, was almost immediate. The hand-shaped beef patties, ground fresh daily, feature a 70/30 meat/fat ratio, ensuring consistently perfect crusts and juicy centers.

Home-cooked everything is the name of the game at Bernie's: scratch condiments, pickles, and hand cut veggies adorn each burger. Turner estimates selling about 4,000 burgers each week at the Bellaire location, surefire evidence they are doing something right.

From food truck roots to a 2016 win on Food Network's cooking competition show *Chopped*, Justin Turner has proven he can pretty much do it all. Turner displays an integrity and conviction in his food, service, and business operations. Moving from his food truck to a series of permanent locations was a big expansion, and unfortunately this resulted in some legal trouble regarding overtime payment to a number of his employees. Turner and his associates made it right, however, reimbursing every last employee affected.

5407 Bellaire Boulevard, Suite A
Houston, TX 77041
713-349-9400, berniesburgerbus.com

Top Left: The kitchen was once a school bus.

Top Right: The lobster roll special is offered every first Friday of each month.

Bottom Left: Condiments like ketchup and mustard made in-house from scratch make all the difference.

Bottom Right: Clever, scholastic-themed menu items continue the school bus tradition.

LES GIVRAL'S SANDWICH & CAFE

Sandwiches are one of the world's great foods. Everybody loves sandwiches. Most cultures and cuisines have some variation of a sandwich, at the very least.

Peking duck is stuffed into steamed buns called bao, usually topped with cucumber and hoisin. That's a sandwich. In England, the chip butty is somewhat of a delicacy. It's basically French fries between two slices of buttered white bread, which perhaps reinforces the stereotype that English food is bland and dull. Still, it's a sandwich. There are heroes, grinders, subs, hoagies, panini, and patty melts.

There is also the the banh mi. In Vietnam, banh mi are usually eaten for breakfast or a light snack. Done well, banh mi are a perfect representation of what a sandwich should be. It all starts with the bread, of course. Warm, crusty baguettes are split sideways, slathered with mayo and pate, and stuffed with crunchy veggies, cilantro, chargrilled meats and spicy jalapeño.

Les Givral's in Midtown does banh mi very well. Evidence of this fact can be easily obtained for the skeptics among us: go to Les Givral's at about 12:30 on a Wednesday afternoon. Odds are the line will be out the door. Almost certainly there will be no place to sit, and there will be about an hour wait for food. Seating is extremely limited inside, as it's a small, narrow restaurant. After such a long wait, people will take their banh mi outside and literally squat on

Be aware that Les Givral's is strictly cash only. Still, it's cheap enough that a tenner buys a meal fit for kings. They also serve excellent Vietnamese coffee.

128

Top Left: Vietnamese coffee, brewed strong. Sweetened condensed milk is added with ice and it all gets shaken together.

Top Right: Spring rolls with shrimp and fresh, bright herbs and veggies. Everything is rolled together with vermicelli and wrapped in chewy rice paper.

Bottom Left: Extreme banh mi close up.

Bottom Right: Order at the counter.

the sidewalk to eat. Hunched over like Gollum, darting their hungry eyes back and forth suspiciously lest someone come for their prize, they'll down their food before scurrying off back to their cubicles.

It's cheap, too.

Everything on the menu is affordable. Banh mi will only set you back a few bucks, and the same goes for bowls of pho. Vermicelli or rice bowls are about $6. Les Givral's light, crunchy spring rolls make a great addition for bigger appetites and are only $2.75 for two.

It's an affordable and delicious lunch spot. Les Givral's is open nightly until 8 p.m., if the lunch madness isn't appealing. Vietnamese food is a smart lunch choice, though. Not overly filling or heavy, a banh mi or rice bowl won't have anybody nodding off at their desks an hour later from food coma.

2704 Milam Street
Houston, TX 77006
713-529-1736

OISHII

As a cuisine, sushi is to Japan as Coca-Cola is to America. Sushi has become synonymous with Japanese food culture to the point where, outside the recent popularity of traditional ramen shops, sushi is simply "Japanese food" for many Americans.

Sushi doesn't actually refer to slices of raw fish, however. The term refers to the particular kind of rice, meticulously prepared and flavored with vinegar. Nigiri is more appropriate terminology for slivers of raw fish, hand-pressed onto balls of sushi rice; maki are hand rolls.

Additionally, "fresh" isn't necessarily terminology Master sushi chefs would use, either. Certain kinds of fish like tuna (toro) are carefully butchered and aged before service. Proper preparation and preservation creates umami, the savory flavor profile imparted by the presence of amino acids called glutamates.

In Japan, sushi is considered an art form. On average, apprenticeships take ten years before one is considered a true chef, the first few years of which are spent cleaning bathrooms, floors, and dishes. Sushi is a cuisine steeped in rules and rituals reflective of Japanese culture as a whole.

In Japanese, oishii means delicious. For example, if someone was eating a particularly good hamburger, they would say "Kono hanbāgā wa totemo oishīdesu." This will not need to be said at Oishii, as they do not serve burgers. As a good rule of thumb, avoid any sushi place that does serve burgers. Additionally, any sushi restaurant offering sushi "on sale" or "buy one get one free" should get a hard pass. Raw fish is absolutely one of those things where you get what you pay for. No one likes an intestinal worm, after all. Affordable is good. Cheap is suspect. Buy one get four free is a death wish.

Left: Kani sunomono. Imitation crab and cucumbers in a tart vinegar sauce. Great starter.

Middle Left: Oishii does peppercorn tuna very well; seared for a crunchy exterior and a kick of spice.

Middle Right: Wasabi tobiko will clear your sinuses. Salmon and tuna are sweet and light. Great sushi is all about balance.

Right: Right out front on a bright, beautiful day.

None of that really matters much at Oishii. One of the best happy hour spots in town, Oishii does not particularly tread heavily on tradition. Happy hour includes cheap Bud Light and French fries. Lacking pretension of any kind seems to be a point of pride, evident in price, patronage, and product.

Familiar elements certainly exist, but sushi places selling onion rings aren't generally putting on any airs.

Oishii's most expensive cuts of fish on menu are affordable, like pieces of sweet shrimp called amaebi or fresh uni, the bright, briny, orange-hued gonads of sea urchins. Crisp, citrusy crab and cucumber sunomono, tempura, dumplings, or basic rolls like California and Spicy Salmon are just a few buy-one-get-one options during happy hour. Fans of wasabi would be smart to order a few pieces of wasabi tobiko, crunchy little flying fish roe turned green from the pungent, spicy, root vegetable.

Weeknight hours between 5 and 7 p.m. find happy hour in full swing. Lines spill out the door, causing long waits, but adroit staff keep things organized. Despite the hubbub, Oishii's servers never rush diners in turning over tables. Such a practice would never happen in Japan, where customers could literally fall asleep at their table and be left utterly alone.

3764 Richmond Avenue
Houston, TX 77046
713-621-8628, oiishihouston.com

KING'S BIERHAUS

According to the city of Pearland, Texas, bratwursts can't legally be distributed at a car wash. Apparently, such practices violate certain local health codes.

All of this was news to Hans Sitter when he opened King's Hand Carwash there in 2009. Hospitality is in his heart, having worked in or around the industry for most of his life. Sitter wanted to give out free brats to guests waiting for their dirty cars. After just a few weeks, Pearland health inspectors shut them down for lacking permits, which is of course brat for business.

So, in 2011, Hans Sitter evolved, opening up the first King's Biergarten in the same lot where his dream of clean cars and full stomachs died just a few years back. Eventually, the place evolved into a large and bustling operation, garnering awards and recognition from local and national press along the way.

A Heights location followed in 2017, as well as a breakfast concept located next door shortly thereafter. As a family, the Sitters are perhaps poorly named, for they seemingly do anything but sit around, idly adjusting their lederhosen straps. Rather, they have partnered with the franchising development group responsible for ushering in brands like Five Guys Burgers and Fries to successful international expansion.

Some of the Sitter's recipes are over 100 years old, tracing back to Hans's Austrian ancestry. Authentic bratwursts and kasewursts (cheese sausages) are house smoked, with natural casings for perfect snap.

Pretzels, Bavarian fried pickles, and smoked wings are precise counterpoints for drinking. Additionally, the menu offers burgers, schnitzels, and a truly tantalizing Hungarian gypsy stew of pork, peppers, and onions in a light paprika sauce.

Exotic sausages of rabbit with rattlesnake, elk, and alligator offer gamier alternatives. And, if they have the energy, vegans have plentiful

Left: GET TO THA CHOPPAH! THERE IS NO TIME!

Middle: Big beers. For about $50 you can get Das Boot, which is a giant glass cowboy boot filled with the beer of your choice.

Right: A selection of sausages, served with bread and mustard.

choices, such as the three artisinal, plant-based links made special for herbivores.

Like any proper biergarten, King's has a wide array of beer options. The "Best Beers in the World" section of the menu is self-explanatory: it features some of the globe's oldest and best brews in massive, half-liter steins. Want to get really wild? Pony up $55 for 'Das Boot,' a commemorative glass cowboy boot filled with 2.5 liters of beer. The mug is a nice memento of something you probably won't remember.

King's Bierhaus worked hard to become a go-to spot for interesting, delicious food, gigantic beers, and two tons of Teutonic fun.

2004 T.C. Jester Boulevard
Houston, TX 77008
281-990-3042, kingsbierhaus.com

BACCO WINE & SPIRITS

Housed in a labyrinthine bungalow, Bacco makes an ideal landing spot for good times.

First off, it's a big place. Bacco has a slew of different rooms outfitted with couches, loungers, love seats, and tables. All the comfort and warmth makes visiting seem like going over to a close friend's house to hang out, and Bacco offers nightly specials that keep patrons coming back, only the friend charges for whatever is ate and drank. That wouldn't be a great friend, of course, but if friends offered the same prices and nightly specials Bacco does, most people wouldn't mind.

Affordable specials include the Tuesday night pizza and wine deal, where ten bucks procures a bottle of wine from a select list or a full pizza. Have both; take your pick. Bacco's pizzas have cracker-like crusts, thin, light, and never egregiously filling, while diverse wine selections cater to all.

It's easy to get physically lost at Bacco, though. This usually occurs after a few too many glasses of wine results in a wayward trip to the bathroom or bar. Still, that's part of the fun.

In truth, it's easier to become existentially lost at Bacco. Time seems to drift away. Even though it's located in one of the city's busiest areas, all the hubbub remains distinctly separate from the effortless, relaxed charm of Bacco. Spending time there is wonderfully serene.

Good food, cheap wine, and soft lighting lull visitors into relaxation, momentarily safe from an otherwise hectic world with food and wine.

5010 Dincans Street
Houston, TX 77005
346-444-5275, baccoteca.com

Left: Specials board. Coming from a former English teacher: whoever wrote this gets an A+ for penmanship. See me after class.

Right: Just one of Bacco's outdoor patios, a comfy spot to chill out and sip some sweet berry wine.

The board reads:

Monday: Burger Night — grilled to order
Tuesday: Any Pizza $10.00 (4-close), select wine bottles $10.00 (18+ only)
Wednesday: Rosé & Any Pizza $24.00
Thursday: Steak/chop Night with select bottle of wine $26.00
Friday: Movie Night — Free popcorn while you watch on Apollo Patio
Saturday: $25.00 Bottles of bubbles
Sunday: Happy Hour ALL day

MALA SICHUAN BISTRO

For the uninitiated, there is one main thing to know about Sichuan cuisine: it's spicy.

Actually, it goes beyond mere Scoville units. Nonetheless, many dishes at Mala Sichuan Bistro are absolutely packed with enough chili peppers to implode someone's lower gastrointestinal tract, like the mapo tofu and red chili oil dumplings. Even their fan-favorite spicy crispy chicken will suffice for hard-core chili heads.

Sichuan peppercorns, though, aren't exactly spicy. They aren't even really that closely related, classification-wise, to black peppercorns or chili peppers. Sichuan peppercorns belong to the citrus family, and rather than burn the tongue, they make it tingle. It's sort of like a super-fizzy soda pop, but without the taste. Eating the little pods, found in many Sichuan dishes, produces a numbing, prickly feeling on the tongue and in the mouth. It's really quite odd, but accompanied by the blast of whole dried chili pods, the resulting effect is unlike anything else.

Mala Sichuan Bistro has operated for years in Chinatown, in yet another strip mall packed with amazing restaurants. In 2015, they opened a second location on Westheimer smack dab in the middle of trendy Montrose. They recruited local sommelier Justin Vinn to craft a sophisticated beer and wine list to pair with the fiery food, as well.

Granted, not everyone wants their mouth set on fire, nor does every diner have an interest in fried pork intestines or stewed beef tendon. Dishes like Kung Pao chicken and the aforementioned red chili oil dumplings are safe(er) options for picky eaters, offering the familiar look and feel of Americanized Chinese food. Still, Mala is anything but Americanized, and they clearly understand how unnecessary it is to do so.

Basically, if your idiot husband loves plain hamburgers and refuses to eat any vegetables, leave him at home.

吃 Street Foods of Sichuan

小熊凉面 House Special Cold Noodle 5.95
ustom made noodles, spiced and chilled, tossed with grinded garlic in an aroma
weet, sour, and mala spicy sesame based vinaigrette, topped with shredded cucum
nd green onions

川担担面 Dan Dan Noodle 5.95
stom made noodle boiled and mixed with mala spicy sauce and sesame paste, topp
n boiled spinach, Yibin preserved vegetables, spiced ground pork, and green onion

肥肠粉 Sour and Spicy Intestine Noodle 4.95
d sweet potato vermicelli in a spicy and sour soup filled with flavorful spices and
il, topped with pork intestines, dry soy beans, spinach, green onions, and Chin
bits

Top Left: Mala's Chinatown storefront.

Top Right: Another house favorite, the red chili oil dumplings.

Above Left: Get the Dan Dan noodles; you won't be disappointed.

Above Right: Outside at the Montrose location.

Vegetarians are in luck at Mala Sichuan. The menu features plenty of meat-free choices. Definitely order the spicy eggplant and Mapo tofu, though, regardless of whether or not meat is out of the picture. Both signature dishes are perfect examples of the balance, heat, and flavor inherent to Sichuan cooking.

In 2017, Chef Jianyun Ye was named a James Beard Award semi-finalist for Best Chef-Southwest. His name was alongside Justin Yu and Hugo Ortega, two of the most well-known and popular chefs in Houston.

It's no surprise, as Mala Sichuan is one of the best restaurants in Houston.

9348 Bellaire Boulevard
Houston, TX 77036
713-995-1889

MELANGE CRÊPERIE

If it was up to Tish Ochoa, her husband Sean Carroll would be running Houston's best snow-cone stand. Instead, he followed his heart and opened a dumb-dumb crepe stand.

"She still hasn't forgiven me," according to Sean.

Carroll moved from Buffalo, New York, to attend the University of Houston, but fell in love with the city. He stayed, working a variety of uninspiring jobs after graduating with an arts background. The final straw came when a supervisor refused to grant him time off for Bills games, so he walked out. Imagine that: quitting a job over the Buffalo Bills. That's a true fan, albeit a delusional one. (Sorry, Sean.)

One day, during one of those hypothetical "what if" conversations most spouses have at some point, Tish asked what he would do if he had a food stand. His answer—the one she still won't forgive him for—was simple.

Crepes.

Beginning with a small push cart and two crepe griddles, known as billigs, Carroll set up shop in a now-defunct bar parking lot at Westheimer and Elgin. Eventually outgrowing his cart, he looked to expand, and after a series of moves, mishaps, and maturations, opened his salmon pink Heights location in 2017. His crepes vary from sweet to savory, drawing inspiration from places like South and Central America, Scandinavia, and Africa.

And they are all delicious.

"Pancake Tacos" is how Carroll describes them to the uninitiated. Not everybody in town knew what the hell a crepe was when he

Blood, water, milk. These three substances are the traditionally accepted liquid ingredients in crepes. Sean doesn't use blood, thankfully. Or does he? Go find out.

Left: The man, the myth, the legend: Sean Carroll pouring up crepes.

Middle: An espresso shot in the beautiful dining room at the Heights Mercantile shopping center.

Top Right: A perfect crepe should be thin enough so that, by holding it close enough, one can almost see through it.

Bottom Right: Nutella; fresh, local strawberries; and sliced banana inside a light and crispy crepe.

started out, but most cultures have something similar to crepes. Melange uses a Southern Britannia recipe, producing thin, slightly sweet crepes with ethereal cracker-crunch edges.

Crepes are French, so let's talk about the French for a second. In pop culture, French people are portrayed as pompous rat bastards, prideful as the day is long and dismissive of all things not French. This is mostly true. However, Carroll has enough experience cooking for real-deal Frenchies, so his staff is trained accordingly. Knowing the regional differences in French crepes allows staff to ask customers which style they would prefer.

Sean Carroll's fans are loyal, as he is a kind, welcoming, magnanimous man. He has a boyish vivaciousness to him, and is at once honest, insightful, and sweet as the Nutella in his crepes. Everyone is greeted warmly when they enter, treated fairly, and fed well.

Crepes are important at Melange, but so is their community.

711 Heights Boulevard, B
Houston, TX 77007
713-393-7578, houstoncrepes.com

THE ORIGINAL NINFA'S ON NAVIGATION

In 1973, at the age of forty-three and mourning the recent, sudden death of her husband, Ninfa Laurenzo did something that permanently changed the course of her family's fortunes. Operating a small tortilla factory in Houston's East End, Ninfa found herself struggling to support her four children. Borrowing money from a family friend, she took a risk and opened a ten-seat restaurant at the front of her factory to increase revenue.

On her menu were two items that were completely new to the Tex-Mex lexicon: salsa verde, a green, tomatillo and avocado puree not regularly featured on Tex-Mex menus at the time, and a dish she called tacos al carbon.

Marinated, grilled, and sliced strips of beef skirt steak were stuffed into her family's homemade, pillowy flour tortillas. She sold 250 tacos al carbon on her first day, inventing what we now know as fajitas, perhaps the most iconic Tex-Mex dish of all time. From there, Mama Ninfa's success grew to towering heights.

Step into the Original Ninfa's today and you will see Mama Ninfa's gift to hungry diners, as smoking, sizzling platters of chicken, beef, and seafood fajitas are ferried across the always-packed open dining room. Executive Chef Alex Padilla quite literally grew up in the kitchens at Ninfa's—his mother was hired by Mama Ninfa as a line cook when he was sixteen, and it was the first experience in a kitchen for the young future chef. After a successful career in some of San Francisco's most-

> "There is an attitude in Texas that makes you feel you can do anything you want to do."
> -Ninfa Laurenzo

Left: Like a welcome beacon in the night. Photos by Lauren Covington.

Right: Chicken and beef combination fajitas. Start with this for a first visit; it's what they're known for.

celebrated eateries, Chef Padilla turned his sights to home, choosing to move back to Houston and take over the kitchen at Ninfa's.

Alba Huerta, who *Texas Monthly* once called "...arguably the best bartender in Texas," curates the cocktail list and drink menu. Along with the Ninfarita, the restaurant's proprietary, original margarita recipe, Huerta offers diners a line of her own signature drinks and margaritas.

Sadly, Ninfa Laurenzo passed away in 2001 at the age of seventy-seven. During the week of her funeral, the Houston City Council postponed their meeting to attend, a testament to her legacy and impact. In 1994, former Mayor Bob Lanier even declared April 13th "Ninfa Laurenzo Day" in honor of her contributions to local education, and an early childhood development school was named after her in 2004.

From humble roots, and through hard work, Mama Ninfa's dream became a cultural landmark, as relevant today as it ever was.

2704 Navigation Boulevard
Houston, TX 77003
713-228-1175, ninfas.com

SAINT ARNOLD BREWING COMPANY

Saint Arnold of Soissons is the patron saint of hop-pickers and beer brewers. One of his 11th century miracles led to canonization by saving countless lives.

Basically, he told people to drink beer instead of water. At the time, disease was rampant. People of this time period didn't understand things like sanitation and medicine, so infectious diseases spread like wildfire. This is still largely the case in Florida.

Drinking beer was much safer, as the brewing process removed those pesky little parasitic microorganisms who love nothing more than seeing their host diarrhea themselves to death. Saint Arnold's advice surely saved many lives, at least in the short run. Most people didn't live long enough to die from liver disease, so drinking beer instead of water kept people safe . . . and drunk.

In Houston, Saint Arnold is still very much revered. As the oldest craft brewery in Texas, Saint Arnold Brewing Company has spread the gospel of hops, creating some of the best beers in the country along the way. Founded by Brock Wagner and Kevin Bartol, Saint Arnold Brewing Company has become one of the largest independent breweries in the region. Unlike some of their beer

Saint Arnold's inside spaces can be rented out for private events. The beer hall can seat up to three hundred people on long picnic tables and is a great place for class reunions, receptions, and parties. In the back, the Investor's Pub can accommodate up to a hundred guests in a smaller, more intimate environment.

Center: Beautifully decorated cars, including the tie-dyed Rolls Royce that posts up for Texans's games.

Left: The many taps, watched over by St. Arnold himself.

Right: Pizza and beer is always a winning combination.

competitors who sold out to the mega-giant corporate overlords, Saint Arnold's remains true to their homebrewing roots.

Their operation moved from their original location to a larger space a few years ago just north of Downtown. In 2018 they added a sizable beer garden and full restaurant, serving pizzas and sandwiches alongside full-format entrees like beer can chicken and grilled salmon or steak. Inside the brewery, the beer hall is open Saturdays for tours and tastings, pouring draughts of their excellent beers and serving a small menu of simple drinking food. Both are great ways to get together with a group of friends or family, enjoy hearty fare, and toss back some local beers.

During football season, Saint Arnold's team drives their tie-died, old-school Rolls Royce down to the football stadium to tailgate Texans games. Attached to the back of the car is a rolling wet bar. They tap a couple kegs and any fan who gets on "the list" early enough in the week can receive a wrist band for some of Saint Arnold's cold, freshly brewed craft beer. Brock Wagner, the founder, sits front row in the endzone section every game. He's always there, rooting for the Texans like everyone else.

200 Lyons Avenue
Houston, TX 77020
713-686-9494, saintarnold.com

LOPEZ

For just over forty years, Lopez has been a Tex-Mex mecca. Located southwest of Houston, close to this author's hometown of Sugar Land, Lopez has never faltered, waivered, or compromised in its quest to provide quality, affordable food every day of the week except Sunday.

When Rodrigo Lopez emigrated from Mexico in 1968, he had no prior business experience. What he did have was moxie and a devoted wife, a recipe for success in any industry. Opening the original location in 1978, Rodrigo's hard work and dedication won the restaurant a loyal fan base. The restaurant has evolved from its humble roots without straying from authenticity. A decades-long series of remodels and expansions have morphed the small, family-run place into its current iteration: an expansive family-run place.

Located just past the Beltway at Wilcrest and Highway 59, visiting during busy weekend nights can be a Mad Max-esque scene in the vast parking lot. Once inside, though, an army of servers, bussers, bartenders, and friendly hostesses move things along at a blistering pace.

Lopez opened a second location in Fort Bend County in 2018. The new restaurant is 7,200 square-feet, located adjacent to Gallery Furniture, a furniture mega store owned by local celebrity and philanthropist Mattress Mack.

Only in Houston would anyone think to buy a recliner and immediately go toss back margaritas and tacos.

ENCHILADAS

Our famous enchiladas topped with Our Signature Chile Gravy Sauce and cheese
Served with rice and beans

ROMA CLASSIC — Two cheese enchiladas 7.95 • Three-add 1.00

CHICKEN OR BEEF — Two Ground Beef or Shredded Chicken 8.95 • Three-add 2.00

FAJITA ENCHILADAS — Two Chicken or Beef Fajita 9.95 • Three-add 2.50

CHILADAS VERDES — Two chicken filled corn tortillas topped with tomatillo sauce, American white cheese, sour cream, and sliced avocados 9.50

ENCHILADAS POPEYE — Two corn tortillas filled with garlic sautéed spinach topped with a creamy mushroom sauce and served with cucumber pico de gallo 8.75

Onions in Enchiladas Unless Requested Otherwise
Small chicken bones may be found in chicken entrees

TEX-MEX COMBOS

Served with Mexican rice and beans

LÓPEZ — Chile relleno, two cheese enchiladas, guacamole salad, beef taco and a chile con queso puff 8.95

OCAMPO — Two cheese enchiladas, beef taco, guacamole salad and a chile con queso puff 10.25

MINA — Two cheese enchiladas, guacamole salad and a beef taco 9.25

HIDALGO — Two cheese enchiladas and a beef taco 8.95

EL TRIO — Choose your favorite three 7.95 Rice and Beans NOT Included
Bean and Cheese Chalupa • Crispy Ground Beef Taco
Cheese Enchilada • Chile Con Queso Puff • Guacamole Salad

Add ground beef or shredded chicken for an additional .85¢ per enchilada.
Add chicken or beef fajita for an additional 1.50 per enchilada.

TEX-MEX FAVORITES

Served with rice and beans

CRISPY TACOS — Three tacos with your choice of ground beef or shredded chicken 7.95

CHIMICHANGA — A deep fried burrito topped with creamy chile con queso. Served with guacamole and sour cream Ground beef 9.75 • Chicken or Beef Fajita 10.50

QUESADILLA — Three lightly toasted flour tortillas filled with cheese and tender chicken or beef fajita. Served with guacamole, sour cream 11.25

BURRITO — Topped with our signature chile gravy sauce. Ground beef 8.50 Carne guisada 8.95 • Chicken or Beef Fajita 9.95

CHALUPAS — Two crispy flat corn tortillas topped with beans, your choice of meat, iceberg lettuce, guacamole, diced tomatoes, shredded cheese and jalapeños Rice and Beans NOT Included
Ground beef 7.95 • Chicken or Beef Fajita 9.50

Left: Lopez's Tex-Mex combos are a great way to explore many of their specialty items.

Top Right: Beef enchiladas smothered in chili con carne and plenty of cheese.

Bottom Right: Chips, salsa, and queso. Everyone always tries not to eat too many chips before the meal, and everyone generally fails.

As a rule, the litmus strip for any Tex-Mex location worth a damn comes down to just three things: chips and salsa, margaritas, and the fajitas. However, Lopez excels elsewhere.

First-timers should opt for a combo plate. The namesake Lopez Combo features a golden brown, crispy chile relleno, two cheese enchiladas, guacamole salad, beef taco, and chile con queso puff, a physics-defying fried corn tortilla crust filled with melted cheese sauce, and all for less than $12.

11606 Wilcrest Drive
Houston, TX 77099
281-495-2436, vivalopez.com

WHATABURGER

There are a few surefire ways to find a fight in Texas. Say that queso is no good, for example. That's an open-handed slap at minimum. Or insult someone's female companion. That's almost assuredly a punch.

Insult someone's mother, though, and all the gods above won't be able to help. That's basically asking to be taken out back and shot.

If fisticuffs aren't on the docket, though, and a heated argument is more your speed, try telling a local that Whataburger sucks. The resulting vitriol aimed in the direction of whoever so utters such blasphemy will be poetic in its outrage.

For many people who grew up in Texas, Whataburger holds a special place in their (clogged) heart.

It was where the team went after a baseball game, win or lose. It's road trip food, and the first stop for many Texans upon returning home. It is where spaced-out high school kids go late at night and attempt to act sober in front of the cops perpetually inside on weekends.

(For the record, kids: the cops know. They totally know. Sober people do not eat three cheeseburgers with a chocolate milkshake at 1 a.m.)

Texas grocery chain H.E.B. carries Whataburger products in their stores. Whataburger Spicy Ketchup is a cut above its crimson competitors. Fans of heat can opt for the Spicy Ketchup. Honey BBQ, Original Mustard, Jalapeño Ranch, and the chain's breakfast pancake mix are also for sale.

Serious fans can go to the company's website for all manner of apparel, and out-of-staters wanting to fill a tiny hole in their hearts can have the crave-worthy condiments shipped direct, however far from home they may be.

Left: Open twenty-four hours; just look for the orange and white.

Middle Left: Officially declared a Texas Treasure by the State Legislature.

Middle Right: A wrapped Whataburger and packet of spicy ketchup.

Right: Ask anyone who went to school in Texas and they will admit to having stolen one of these numbers at some point in their life.

Whataburger basically is Texas, ever since 1950 when Harmon Dobson opened the first store in Corpus Christi. As the story goes, when new customers would eat Dobson's beefy creations, they couldn't help but exclaim "What a burger!" Big, bright, orange-and-white color schemes at each location lure pot bellies and ample posteriors all the way from El Paso to Texarkana like moths to a flame.

Perhaps it goes without saying that, of course, Whataburger serves burgers—really good ones.

The patties are thin, griddled on a flat top and slapped into a five-inch bun. A double burger with cheese is a magnificently filling gut bomb. I once watched a friend eat a triple patty burger with three slices of cheese, grilled onions, bacon, and jalapeños. He basically slept for two days after that. Whataburger also offers a famous breakfast menu, and loyal fans can be downright ornery if they are unable to make it during breakfast hours between 11 p.m. and 11 a.m. Others swear by the chicken tenders, served with cream gravy thicker than a bowl of oatmeal.

Expansion has made Whataburger the country's eighth largest burger chain, and staying open twenty-four hours a day provides ample chance to see exactly why it's so popular.

Multiple Locations
1-800-628-7437 (Customer Service Line), whataburger.com

THE PASS & PROVISIONS

Technically, the Pass & Provisions are two separate restaurants. Upstairs, the Pass is a much smaller and more intimate (read: expensive) dining experience—nightly high-concept, prixe-fixe tasting menus are developed by the immensely talented team. Menus at the Pass change fairly regularly, always offering innovative creations. Diners choose between an omnivore or all-vegetarian set menu. Meals are served in either five or eight courses while supplemental beverage pairings from the bar team complement each course. Drinks are always esoteric but precisely paired for each course and flavor profile, whether it's dessert wine or rare spirit.

On the first floor, Provisions serves more rustic, familiar a la carte items and a full bar. Pasta, pizza, salads, and great wine with friends—that kind of thing. It's gourmet but pleasantly unpretentious. Lunch, brunch, and happy hour are served; a ground floor bar and patio both make cozy spots to loosen up before dinner. Or skip dinner. Just have some more wine. No judgement; just don't be a dillweed: call a cab.

Do not, however, conflate Provisions's more accessible price point with reduction in quality or execution.

Refrain from such thinking, as it would be a gross miscalculation.

Provisions's cresta di gallo, one of Houston's best pasta dishes, is made of ridged, tubular little arches of house-made pasta and paired with hen-of-the-woods mushrooms in a complex, light, foamy broth of parmesan and roasted yeast. It's earthy, umami, and exquisite.

The large, multi-level location formerly housed legendary Houston deli shop Antone's Po'Boys, but Chef/Owners Terrence Gallivan and Seth Siegel-Gardner have distinctly created their own local legend with the Pass & Provisions. James Beard nominations and awards have been plentiful, but arguably the love and loyalty of their hungry guests is what's kept them successful since opening in 2013. Both

he original Antone's Deli is gone but not forgotten. 50 years
ago the Antone's Import company opened and helped change
the way Houstonians eat. This menu pays homage to the
business that started it all.

MENU
DAILY 2:30PM - 6:00PM

FOOD
(DINE-IN ONLY)

ORIGINAL PO' BOY"
D BY THE ORIGINAL ANTONES
ADELLA/CAPOCOLLA/
OLONE/MAYO/CHOW
PEPPER RELISH/L/T
10

READ & BUTTER 4

HAM O DAY 8

DRINKS

MARGARITA 6
tequila, lime, orange

OLD FASHIONED 6
rye, bitters, demerara

MOSCOW MULE 6
vodka, aperol, ginger beer

PROVISIONS

Left: Happy hour menu, paying homage to the Original Antone's Po'Boys. Inside Provisions's dining room is a bright yellow Antone's sign.

Top Middle: A clever and simple branding with double Ps, one for each restaurant.

Top Right: Cresto di gallo. A beautiful dish.

Bottom Right: Provisions menu featuring a circle of seafood.

restaurants were collectively voted sixth on Bon Appetit's Best New Restaurants in America list the same year, which certainly also helps.

Gallivan and Seigel-Gardner have experience and lots of it, all the way to the loftiest peaks of the industry. They met in 2005 during stints running Gordon Ramsay's New York City restaurant Maze.

Whether it's an expense account blowout, relaxed and intimate dinner, or drinks and a snack after work, the Pass & Provisions does it all and then some. Consistently high-quality service and food have kept this combination concept as fresh and relevant as when the doors opened for the very first time.

807 Taft Street
Houston, TX 77019
713-628-9020, passandprovisions.com

THE HOBBIT CAFE

Hairy feet, squat stature, and love of second breakfast aren't prerequisites for dining at the Hobbit Cafe. Nor is a crew of boisterous dwarves or distaste for adventure either. In fact, diners need not even be fans of J.R.R. Tolkien's fantasy world of Middle-Earth. While fandom helps for appreciation of the clever, book-inspired menu item names and the plentiful Tolkien memorabilia that makes up the décor, it's not needed to still have a good meal.

When the Hobbit Hole Cafe opened its original location in 1972, the menu was entirely unique for Houston at the time, serving strictly vegetarian cuisine. This trend continued for ten years, though the restaurant eventually relented to Texans' taste for meat, like orcs do for man flesh.

By 1998, the "Hole" was dropped and the Hobbit Cafe had relocated to its current location at Kirby and Richmond. A re-tooled menu was developed, adding wine and a plentiful beer selection, including fifteen draft brews and well over 100 bottle and can options.

The Hobbit Cafe's sizable outdoor deck, shaded by the verdant foliage of a massive oak tree, makes a perfect place to enjoy a pint

It's a little-known fact that Tolkien wrote the *Lord of the Rings* intending for it to be published as a single, massive book. However, the narrative was split into three books, first published in 1954. Printing costs were sky-high due to paper shortages after the war, so it simply was impractical to publish a massive single volume. Tolkien still considered it a single work, and it's best read as such. Impress your dining companions at the Hobbit Cafe with this fascinating and utterly useless tidbit of literary history.

Lots of trees enhance the Middle-Earth theme, though Tom Bombadil won't come to the rescue if one of them wakes up angry.

and sandwich for elevenses, lunch, afternoon tea, or any of the other seven meals Hobbits traditionally consume each day. And vegetarians can still be delighted irrespective of the meat items, because even the most ardent of plant-based dieters have choices aplenty.

Sandwiches like the Hobbit Cafe's Gandalf, featuring a massive layer of avocado topped with mushrooms and melted jack cheese, are filling and delicious. Thorin Oakenshield, the leader of Bilbo's party in *The Hobbit* and redemptive hero of the book's "Battle of Five Armies" finale has a namesake sandwich featuring fresh, house-made tabbouleh, more avocado, tomato, sprouts, and a touch of mayo.

The Hobbit Cafe's sandwiches are delicious, to be sure, but carnivores up for a challenge can tangle with a horror from the deep, a demon from the ancient world.

Balrog.

A massive mound of two half-pound burger patties, the Balrog is topped with double cheese, bacon, avocado, stuffed jalapeño, mushrooms, sliced jalapeño, and chipotle mayo. It is a worthy foe, one not easily thrown down to smite the mountainside with its ruin. Regular, human-sized alternative burgers are on the menu, too, like black bean and salmon.

Open for lunch, dinner, and brunch, the Hobbit Cafe is a fun and healthy place, accommodating dietary needs for hobbit, man, or elf.

2243 Richmond Avenue
Houston, TX 77098
713-526-5460, hobbitcafehtx.com

Left: "A great smoke rose about us, vapour and steam. Ice fell like rain. I threw down my enemy, and he fell from the high place and broke the mountain-side where he smote it in his ruin." —Gandalf the White.

Right: I'm going on an adventure!

THE PASTRY WAR

Unfortunately, pastry lovers need to look elsewhere if they actually want pastries. It says so right on the brief menu of bar snacks sold at the Pastry War.

Tamales, chips, salsa, and queso are offered, as well as Tajin-spiced pineapple served with Mexican peanuts. The Pastry War, though, is a bar first and foremost, the brainchild of cocktail maestros Alba Huerta and Bobby Heugel. Focusing on spirits derived from agave, the bar self-identifies as a 'mezcaleria,' which is perhaps a new term to some. Between the two, Huerta and Heugel are involved in some of Houston's most successful and esteemed high-end cocktail bars.

At the Pastry War, the focus is on Mexican drinking culture, thoroughly honored by serving one of the best margaritas in town. Carefully selected tequilas and mezcals from small, family-run Mexican distillers directly results from the founders personally visiting each producer. They have compiled an extensive, incredible listing of tequila and mezcal to sample. Such commitment has produced a vast array of remarkable things to get drunk on.

Excuse me: I meant to say "a vast array of remarkable, hand-crafted and selected spirits to sample responsibly."

However one chooses to justify their drinking, what isn't up for debate is how tasty the options for going about it are. Margaritas de la Casa, which can be ordered shaken or frozen, are made with lime, tequila, agave nectar, and garnished with citrus salt. Additional flavorings can be added in, like strawberry for sweetness or chili peppers for extra kick.

310 Main Street
Houston, TX 77002
713-225-3310, thepastrywar.com

Left: Margarita and some excellent mezcal de pechuga, made with actual, 100% raw chicken breast. Ask them about it.

Right: The entrance to the Pastry War doesn't necessarily stand out. The drinks, however, do.

HK DIM SUM

Dim sum isn't a meal for one.

Well, it should not be such a meal, at least. It would be weird, and there is a distinct possibility of not getting seated promptly—or at all.

It's a dining experience, like Korean barbecue, hot pot, or tapas. Basically, dim sum is tapas, just the Chinese version. Small bites of food are served in steaming tins or small plates meant for sharing.

Selection, sharing, and variety are at the heart of places like HK Dim Sum in Houston's Chinatown. It's a wonderful, relatively inexpensive way to explore this ancient cuisine.

Starting centuries ago along the Silk Road, yum cha is the historical basis for dim sum, where weary traders were offered tea and snacks at pit stops along the way. The more modern iterations owe their roots to Canton. Today, it is still a form of dining that is almost ritualistic. Many dim sum shops in China and Hong Kong open even before dawn; older crowds often flock to satiate their post-morning exercise hunger pangs.

Dishes like a steamed shrimp dumpling with thin wrapping called har gao, chicken feet, Chinese broccoli with oyster sauce, and the ubiquitous egg roll can all be found at HK Dim Sum.

However, they break from tradition in a few ways. Mainly: no rolling carts. The restaurant is far too small for loaded steam carts passing by to order from. Diners use pencils to check boxes on paper menus, and servers bring all the food out fresh.

9889 Bellaire Avenue, #110
Houston, TX 77072
713-777-7029, hkdimsumcity.com

Top: Signage. Expect to wait, especially on weekends.

Bottom Left: Fill out the form to order.

Bottom Right: Steamed shrimp dumplings. Best with vinegar sauce and chili oil.

People from Philly can be angry as a kicked hornet nest when it comes to their hometown.

For instance, Veterans Stadium, the Eagles' former NFL home field, was forced to install a holding tank and sitting judge for unruly fans. In a single Monday Night Football Game in 1998, there were almost twenty fistfights in the stands. Suffice it to say that wearing an opposing team's jersey at a Philly sports game will result in at least a black eye or two.

Afterwards, though, it's all about the cheesesteaks.

Possibly no other city in America has a food as ubiquitous and immediately recognizable as the Philly cheesesteak. Buffalo has its wings. Chicago has its deep-dish pizza. New Orleans has gumbo and po' boys.

The City of Brotherly Love may be known as the birthplace of our nation, but it's just as well known for fluffy hoagies stuffed with griddled steak bits smothered in imitation cheese sauce. The Philly cheesesteak is often imitated but rarely replicated. Indeed, natives of Philly are downright contentious about this fact. Most won't even bother eating one outside the city. A perfect cheesesteak is a melty and cheesy gut bomb of grease, yet Philly residents are discerning when it comes to quality.

Mostly, it comes down to the bread.

Like New Yorkers, whose sense of superiority regarding pizza and bagels is founded in their dirty water, proper cheesesteak bread is an exact science. It should have a brittle outside crust but silken inside crumb for absorbing sizzling meat, cheese, and onion juices.

Every Papa Geno's location around Houston has this same hardscrabble, no-nonsense mantra. Rolls are flown in fresh from a Buffalo, New York, bread purveyor. Though their steaks have a decidedly Southern addition of mayo, it is pure sandwich art.

Look for the orange and white checkers and cheesesteaks will be found.

The menu even features subs inspired by the food truck trend in Philly of "fat" sandwiches, overstuffed with fried mozzarella sticks, chicken tenders, French fries, and brown gravy. Papa Geno's Wicked Philly features all of these ingredients, plus a topping of a giardiniera, combining a Texas twist of jalapeños in the pickled mix. And, of course, the cheese sauce is spelled with a 'Z' and comes in a can. Provolone is fine, but a true cheesesteak needs its cheese sauce to bind everything together.

Papa Geno's sandwiches provide a perfectly proportioned slice of East Coast tradition with a generous side of Down South hospitality.

Multiple Locations
713-863-1222 (Heights Location), papagenos.com

NAM GIAO

Most of the time, when the average diner thinks of Vietnamese food what comes to mind fits into a fairly familiar mold: banh mi, pho, spring rolls, and rice plates. Lots of vermicelli noodles, plenty of lemongrass and peanut sauce. These dishes, and their flavor and texture, are recognizable and friendly to Western palates.

Nam Giao is something definitely a little different, an opportunity to broaden one's culinary horizons.

This isn't the simple, rustic soups and rice plates one can find just anywhere. Here, they serve Hue cuisine, known as the food of royalty in Vietnam. Hue was an ancient capital city during Vietnam's final feudal period, the Nguyen Dynasty.

The menu is large, and while there are some of the more standard items to choose from, Nam Giao shines brightest with their house specialties. Listed on the very front of the menu is "Our Distinctive Appetizers," the crown jewels of Hue cooking, and what Nam Giao does best.

Imagine a fusion between tapas and dim sum, but with the flavors of Vietnam. At first, the textures of some dishes may seem odd to newcomers, but the refinement and artistry of their presentation will assuage any uncertainty. Delicate pork and shrimp dumpling in paper-thin wrappings or steamed rice cakes with chopped shrimp and carrots served in little platters are perfect bites. Or, try the minced shrimp, wrapped around sugarcane and chargrilled.

Words fail to capture Nam Giao's flavorful, addictive, authentic cuisine.

It's fit for an emperor, which says it all.

6938 Wilcrest Drive, Suite C
Houston, TX 77072
281-568-4888

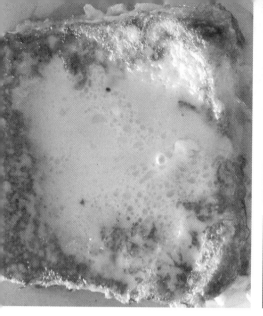

Top Left: Hong Kong–style French toast, topped with sweetened condensed milk.

Top Right: Combo fried rice. Look at them shrimps!

Bottom Right: They have plates, too. Just saying.

OPORTO FOODING AND WINE HOUSE

Portugal often gets overlooked.

Spain is more famous. France basically invented cooking. Italy produced pizza and pasta. England perfected fish and chips, shepherd's pie, and the horrors of imperialism.

All these countries garner more accolades than oft-forgotten Portugal, but what it lacks in stateside status is made up for in substance. A rich history of trade and maritime dominance, coupled with Islamic influences from Moorish rule, produced a culture and cuisine with lasting impact on how the world eats.

By about the 16th century, for example, Portuguese traders and missionaries brought chili peppers to Korea and introduced tempura frying to Japan. Such travel and trade likewise introduced different ingredients into Portugal, including many types of olives, nuts, and grapes. In fact, Portugal has over 300 grape varietals, the vast majority of which only exist there. Portuguese wine is somewhat rare, however, because not very much gets exported. The good stuff can only be found there.

Which is exactly what makes Oporto Fooding House & Wine such a standout star in the dining world. The Midtown location has an extensive wine list that includes many such delicious, rare Portuguese wines and comprehensive, inventive menus. Oporto serves meals

> The Di Virgilios also operate Oporto Café, their original location in a strip center at Richmond and Buffalo Speedway. Smaller and much more intimate, Oporto Café has many similarities, but the sprawling dining room at Oporto in Midtown, replete with beautiful lighting and an open kitchen, is a far more elaborate affair.

Left: A broccoli and ricotta pizza.

Middle: Start the meal right with some bubbly inspiration.

Right: Seafood balchão curry, served with rice and naan.

worth lingering over. It's a shared-plates experience, best with groups. However, couples seeking romantic evenings are also in luck, too.

Like any wine-centric menu, meat and cheese are prime starting points. Oporto's house-made octopus salami is a curious twist definitely worth trying. Iberico ham, shaved fresh from the hock, possesses rich, earthy flavor profiles from the pig's acorn-only diet. There are ample cheese selections, and the crispy crackers included are perfect textural contrasts.

Chefs and owners Rick Di Virgilio and his wife Shiva have drawn upon their own cultures to create something truly special at Oporto. Rick's Italian and Portuguese family ties and Shiva's Indian heritage marry all over again on each plate. Curry, salted cod fritters, or scallops over a turmeric-laden risotto are favorites. Finger foods like crab and avocado crostini or crispy, smashed fingerling potatoes make perfect starters.

Weekday lunch and weekend brunches at Oporto are just as decadent and delicious. For dinner, larger-format entrees satisfy larger appetites. Pizzas, paella, flaming Portuguese sausages, and beef tenderloin skewers topped with dabs of herbed butter can feed whole tables.

Or, go for happy hour, which runs from 3 to 6:30 p.m. each weekday, a fun way of sampling Oporto's uncommonly good food and wine.

125 West Gray, #500
Houston, TX 77019
713-528-0115, oportomidtown.us

Texans are not much for change, particularly when it comes to the foundational aspects of living here. This commitment to ritual is almost fanatical in the barbecue world of Texas.

We love our barbecue. Things don't change much here, nor does it happen quickly. History holds a special place in every Texan's heart. We don't forget the Alamo.

It is tradition. Traditions are cherished in Texas. As such, it's difficult to be innovative with barbecue.

This remains partly true due to a by-the-book bent of many pit masters. Things are usually done how things have always been done when smoking meat. Texas barbecue is a religious experience, part of our cultural heritage, like cowboys, gravy, guns, trucks, and all the songs about trucks. (For the uninitiated, check out George Strait's classic country song "Take Me to Texas" for an idea of our devotion to the Lone Star State.)

The Pit Room stands out from its barbecue brethren, adhering to norms while departing in remarkably stunning ways. For instance, Tex-Mex influence found its way onto the menu. Fat from smoked brisket is rendered into lard, used in scratch-made flour tortillas for chicken, pork, and brisket tacos.

Pit Room tacos stand apart from the adhered-to barbecue status quo, particularly the chicken. Whole cloves of smoked garlic layer caramelized sweetness and pungency with smoked, shredded chicken, griddled cheese, and green salsa. It's a dish harmonizing with itself, like the pentatonic call of a Peruvian throat singer.

A raw bar of taqueria-worthy condiments awaits every loaded tray coming off the serving line. Escabeche-style vegetables in a piquant cure sit next to pickled red onions, salsas, and bog standard selections of raw white onion, jalapeños, and dill pickle. Charro

Top Left: Meat: sausages and beef ribs.

Top Right: Condiment bar and lots of sauce options.

Bottom: Two-meat plate with mac and cheese, coleslaw, turkey, and brisket.

beans supplement the Mexican influences while coleslaw or mac and cheese satisfy the standard sides.

But, let's talk about beef ribs. Most of us, even barbecue aficionados, don't regularly partake in beef ribs. Most places don't even regularly serve them—they are often relegated to special days of the week due to availability and price. The Pit Room breaks with this norm, as well. Gargantuan beef ribs bathe in smoke for long hours, producing a dense bark that crunches into a superb center. The barbecue equivalent of filet mignon, The Pit Room's rectangular haunch of beef rib can be deftly flicked from the bone with a butter knife, rendering useless the pointed tines of a fork.

1201 Richmond Avenue
Houston, TX 77006
291-888-1921, thepitroombbq.com

TACOS TIERRA CALIENTE

O wning a restaurant is not particularly easy. Fickle, internet-review driven customers pair nicely with a market constantly in flux, resulting in a persnickety industry oft tethered to trendy ingredients and whims of self-important bloggers. I should know: I used to be a self-important blogger.

Now, I am a self-important author and obviously trustworthy, so trust when I say Tacos Tierra Caliente has the best tacos on either side of the Mason-Dixon. Conducting business for almost two decades from a beat-up trailer, this mom-and-pop spot serves something special—barbacoa, addictive, crimson al pastor, and fall-apart *lengua* are some of the meats scooped into homemade tortillas Mexican street style, *con cilantro y cebollas*. Gargantuan stuffed *tortas* with avocado, mayo, lettuce and tomato on puffy bread are simply beyond measure, regardless of meat choice. Taste buds will be tested by the house salsas, but both creamy green and firey red versions should be liberally splashed on everything.

And it's cheap. Tortas are $5, flour tortillas are $2, corn is $1.50; quesadillas with enough cheese to constipate a small army are a measly $3.50. Breakfast tacos served until the oddly-specific hour of 11:40 a.m. are only $1.

Do not let price point confound quality. Only fools assume such things. The truck's ponderous, worn exterior belies how good it is. Located across from West Alabama Ice House, a legendary watering hole, Tacos Tierra Caliente punches above weight class in accolade.

Awards and press abound at this humble neighborhood eatery: 7th best tacos in America by Business Insider, Top 10 Tacos in Texas by

---

"Tamales Tamales Tamales!" If you hear this, get them.

Left: Tamales, salsa, and beer. The combination of these things and nice weather is testament to just how good life can be.

Right: As mentioned, there are plenty of onions and cilantro for that Mexican street-style flavor. Drown it all in red and green salsa.

Yelp, and regularly honored in Best-Of lists from local press, among others. Long lines of half-buzzed drinkers waiting for orders are testament to greatness, but the community's response once tragedy struck in 2016 truly displayed owner Maria Victoria's influence. Houston takes care of its own. It was obvious after Harvey, but living here day-to-day makes apparent the kindness and concern Houstonians have for each other.

Maria's daughter died too young at twenty-two, but despite their success, the family struggled to pay medical and funeral costs. Neighboring West Alabama Ice House started a GoFundme to help, easily tripling the original goal of $5,000 in less than one day.

Cash only, Tacos Tierra Caliente is an iconic and nationally recognized institution by no small measure. Grab some beers at the Ice House and enjoy America's best tacos.

2003 W. Alabama Street
Houston, TX 77098
713-584-9359

JAMES CONEY ISLAND (JCI GRILL)

Although re-branded in 2013 to JCI Grill, Houstonians know this local chain only by its original name: James Coney Island. James Coney Island has been serving Coney-style hot dogs for close to eighty years.

Started by brothers Tom and James Papadakis in 1923 as a downtown food stand, James Coney Island has grown to twenty-one successful locations around town. Sons of a carpenter from Kastelli Gravias, Greece, the brothers began when James was convinced by his brother Tom—equipped with $75 and a third grade education—to sell hot dogs for a nickel, bowls of "secret recipe" chili for $.15, and "goose liver and Roquefort" sandwiches, now thankfully off the menu.

They were met with immediate success. In fact, overflow from long lunch lines were seated at wooden school desks placed out front the original location at Walker and Main, a motif that didn't change for many years, just like their best seller: hot dogs stuffed in steamed-soft buns, layered with thin, red chili and a cheese sauce.

Today, customers can find a menu that has expanded from its humble roots; however the Coney dogs still use the famous original chili recipe to top their toothsome, snappy dogs. The mustard and minced onions are optional. JCI, as it is now known, does seasonal dogs, and other "elevated" versions of the humble frankfurter. In the past local chefs like Matt Marcus and Chef Hori from Kata Robata have created their own gourmet dogs, all much better than dad's rubbery microwaved version.

Multiple Locations
713-932-1500 (Support Center number), jamesconeyisland.com

Left: Coney dogs, sans onions.

Right: I frankly refuse to look up what the official name of this mascot is, so I will call him Lil'
Red Weiner Man.

John Peterson started The Rice Box food truck in 2011. Peterson just wanted diners to be reminded of the takeout-style Chinese we have all grown to know and love: white boxes with red Chinese characters, familiar menu choices, and "the best General Tso's chicken" around.

When Peterson opened his second stand-alone location in the Heights, his dream came to fruition. After critical acclaim from locals, food critics, and even an appearance on Food Network's mobile eatery show Eat Street, he closed food truck operations in 2017.

Still, the food will definitely resemble standard Chinese-American staples, like sweet and sour chicken in corn syrup red sauce, broccoli beef, sesame chicken, and fried rice. These familiar dishes are refined, but still reminiscent of the mom-and-pop restaurants found in strip malls and shopping centers, with names featuring some combination of the words "Panda," "Lotus," "Garden," or "Bamboo." Family run joints where there is always a little girl in the corner doing her homework.

Thankfully, Peterson isn't lying about having the best General Tso's around. The Rice Box General Tso's, featuring a crunchy rice flour breading coated in a spicy-sweet sauce and dotted with dried red chills, is a nostalgic revelation. The menu has all the hits, like golden-fried egg rolls so crispy they splinter when bitten into. One egg roll comes with every order, but get two. Order extra plum sauce, as well—the kind in little plastic rectangular packaging that never seems to tear open just right. The dumplings, accompanied by a spicy soy dipping sauce, are the perfect companion to any entree.

The Heights Rice Box is Peterson's second brick-and-mortar outpost, but is definitely the way to go, as his love for sci-fi films inspired a decor paying homage to the White Dragon Noodle Bar

Top Left: Always busy, but the counter service is impeccable.

Top Right: The Rice Box has a super cool, sleek design.

Bottom Left: Taps, soy sauce, and sriracha.

Bottom Right: Close up of the General Tso's chicken with fried rice, broccoli, and crunchy cabbage.

from Blade Runner. Step into this futuristic spot, replete with neon-lighting and polished metal counters, and you will half expect Decker to be downing chow fun next to you. The other location underneath Greenway Plaza has limited hours, but still serves workers and out-of-town clients white collar power lunches during business hours.

Elbow in and pull up a seat at the counter. Order a beer, and dig into elevated Chinese takeout fare, the kind that you ate as a kid, and later ordered after a night of heavy drinking in college. Both locations offer the same skillfully prepared food. Or have it delivered from an app-based service.

300 West 20th Street
Houston, TX 77008
281-305-8555, riceboxed.com

Absolutely do not order a Lone Star Light in the Lonestar State. Absolutely not. Do not do that.

Since 1884 Lone Star has been brewed in Texas. It is the National Beer of Texas, as much a part of the local diet as air and water. Lone Star is, in fact, the perfect barometer for understanding most kinds of places here in Texas. For the sake of comparison, precisely how Lone Star is priced, served, and consumed can tell an individual a great deal about an establishment.

For example, if Lone Star is expensive, you should leave.

Anything over $5 is expensive—and that is for tall boys, too. High-end restaurants and wine bars who serve $4 Lone Star know the score, same as any open-air ice house with the same price point. After closing, staff from both places will likely end up at a hole-in-the-wall dive serving the same can of beer for $2.

Looking to make a good first impression at a tailgate or backyard barbecue? Bring a big case of Lone Star, and make sure it's the camouflage-colored cans. Because yes, they have those, and yes, it's as awesome and tacky as it probably sounds. Underneath each bottle cap on glass longnecks of Lone Star are little pictograph riddles, which can be fun in a wildly frustrating kind of way.

"It's Thursday and it's past noon. Thursday is one of my days off. On my days off I start drinking at noon. You don't get to interrupt that."

–Rust Cohle, cracking open a Lone Star on HBO's hit show *True Detective*

Top Left: Texas Two-Step; a shot of bourbon and a Lone Star.

Right: Why yes, more Lone Star. This photo was taken in the back of Rudyard's, where most of this book was written.

Bottom Left: Typical Lone Star advertisement—and prices—at the West Alabama Ice House.

Lone Star can be ordered in a dingy bar or fancy steakhouse, and odds are it'll cost the same. For sure it will taste the same. You know, like beer.

Roost is surprising.

It's surprising such elegant and refined food comes from such a tiny kitchen. It's surprising how relaxing Roost is, how effortlessly laid back and cozy a meal can be. It's utterly unpretentious yet upscale. Service is prompt but never pushy, with an almost European approach to dining out.

What's most surprising is irrespective of how celebrated, well-reviewed, and beloved Roost has become, it continues to happily create new surprises.

There is an identity and purpose to what Chef Kevin Naderi and his team have accomplished at Roost. When he opened his own restaurant for the first time in 2011 Chef Naderi was only twenty-six, but he borrowed from his experiences working in New York, Napa, and Houston. His tremendous talent and knowledge pushed Naderi to create curious, complex menus. Roost manages to somehow be eclectic and focused in equal measure.

Menus change every four to six weeks, keeping things fresh and seasonal. Certain dishes are menu stalwarts, however, such as Roost's famous fried cauliflower. Removal of this fan favorite would be calamitous.

Flash fried and topped with a miso dressing, pine nuts, scallions, and dancing bonito flakes, it's the kind of appetizer capable of outshining most entrees. A desert of coffee donut holes with caramel ice cream remains similarly omnipresent on Roost's menu.

Roost doesn't take reservations for fewer than parties of six, but has a pleasant, relaxed feel and the front patio makes waiting with discounted beer and wine manageable—if not downright enjoyable—during a pre-dinner happy hour.

It's a neighborhood place, comfortable and welcoming. A small but thoughtful beer and wine list rounds out the artful food.

Left: Giant breadtzel, for lack of a better word—part bread, part pretzel; totally delicious. Served in this picture with homemade pimento cheese butter, chicken schmaltz (fat) butter, and lemon-pear butter.

Middle Top: Local herb in a cute little candleholder alongside the wine list.

Top Right: The famous fried cauliflower, so popular that Roost never lets it leave the menu. For good reason, too.

Bottom Right: Italian basil panna-cotta with watermelon ice, candied basil seeds and aged balsamic syrup, a perfect summer dessert.

Roost's bread service, a giant pretzel paired with trios of continually evolving compound butters, is a delectable starter or complementary order. Entrees and larger-format dishes are at the upper end of the restaurant's price point, but cost-wise Roost is a far cry from some of the higher-end fine dining establishments in Houston.

With only fifty seats and relatively small menus, Roost obviously puts a great deal of focus into the details. From the decor to the dessert menu, every base is covered, every plate is seasoned, and every customer is treated to warm and friendly service. Roost makes every dish a well-engineered labor of love, and the staff members clearly carry a passion and commitment for what they are doing.

If they served pudding, the proof would be in it.

1972 Fairview Street
Houston, TX 77006
713-523-7667, Iloveroost.com

LA GUADALUPANA

In ancient times, cinnamon was near priceless. Roman encyclopedist Pliny the Elder mentioned cinnamon's significance in his comprehensive, thirty-seven–volume *Naturalis Historia*. By AD 77, a Roman pound of cinnamon cost 1,500 dinarii—roughly fifty months, wages—a gift for royalty or the gods.

At La Guadalupana, it flavors every cup of coffee. Fortunately, Trancito Diaz, chef and owner, doesn't require noble parentage. From a corner spot in a tiny shopping center with a convenience store and washateria, this nondescript cafe serves divine Mexican breakfast.

Mr. Diaz's brother produces La Guadalupana's sui generis coffee in Puebla, Mexico, their native land. Whole cinnamon plants are roasted alongside the beans, infusing essential oils and flavor.

As a result, walking past in the morning is a struggle, if not an outright impossibility to the weak willed. Thanks to the aromas of hot, fresh churros from the fryer and cinnamon coffee, visiting becomes an absolute must.

Formerly a baker at a country club, then a catering company, Mr. Diaz developed his skills with confectionaries early on. Tres leches, almond croissants, and the aforementioned churros filled with thick, sweet dulce de leche sit behind a glass cooler next to the register. Hungry eyes betray even faithful dieters who gaze upon these tempting delicacies.

Go ahead. Give in. Treat yourself.

Sweets and coffee are far from everything La Guadalupana has to offer. It isn't consistently rated among the city's best restaurants by accident, irrespective of the rickety plastic tables and chairs. Mr. Diaz's binder of recipes is a collection of comforting, authentic Mexican dishes.

Strips of tortillas fried firm and doused in salsa, otherwise known as chilaquiles, can be topped with any of the restaurant's meat

Top Left: Migas all day.

Top Middle: Coffee and a convenience store. That's brunch, baby.

Bottom Left: The charming exterior.

Right: Huevos rancheros, a meal fit for kings and royal hangovers alike.

options or eggs. Oil, tortillas, and spicy sauce combine to combat any ailment, be it common cold or hangover.

For serious hangovers, order menudo. And I don't mean the Latin boy band sensation that launched Ricky Martin's career. Rather, menudo is a hangover panacea: soup cooked with beef tripe, hominy, and red chili. What's better for upset stomachs than eating stomach? Because that's what tripe is—spongy and chewy cow stomach, cooked in long-simmered broth. Huevos rancheros and machaca norteña can—and should—be ordered whenever.

La Guadalupana remains open until 3 p.m. to accommodate late breakfasts and sparse lunch crowds. Weekends are hectic. Both seating and parking are limited, but Mr. Diaz's family, including restaurant manager Roberto Diaz, Trancito's son, help run things.

2109 Dunlavy Street
Houston, TX 77006
713-522-2301

RUDYARD'S BRITISH PUB

Full disclosure: Rudyard's is my *Cheers.*
And yes, (mostly) everybody knows my name. However, first timers to Rudyard's may experience mild cognitive dissonance once walking through the door. Whereas patrons may imagine a traditional British public house—plush booths and sophisticated gentlemen in tweed jackets speaking the Queen's English over fish and chips—the reality couldn't be further from the truth. It's the self-styled "Living Room of Montrose" for a reason.

Rudz, as it's known by regulars, is kind of a dive bar.

There are definitely excellent fish and chips, but the best-selling item at this legendary Montrose bar is their cheeseburger, unequivocally ranking among the city's best. The classic Rudz burger is an expertly prepared carnivore's delight: griddled, slightly sweet buns bookend a peppery, crusty patty grilled to juicy medium inside, and topped with fresh salad stuff with a swipe of mayo.

Diners have the option of fries or tater tots, but a glance at the other bar-goers reveals the truth: the tot is king at Rudz. Crispy, salty, golden-fried perfections of potato pair perfectly with the meaty burger.

Visitors can order a daily lunch special consisting of burger, fries or tots, and a beer for around ten bucks every day until 2 p.m. and all day Sundays.

Rudyard's has a full menu with different burger options, including a veggie patty for non-meat eaters—a well-executed alternative to its red meat cousin. There are also fried foods for soaking up any of the thirty-eight beers on tap, spirits, and a memorable Bloody Mary.

Upstairs is a venue featuring live music, spoken word, and a great, local open-mic comedy show every Monday. BooTown, a non-profit local performance and theater group, hosts a monthly series

Left: Outside Rudyard's, located at Waugh and Welch in the very heart of Montrose.

Middle Top: Regular barfly Barksdale with her handler, Greg. Just playing some shuffleboard.

Middle Bottom: Clear through the bar, all the way to the dart boards.

Top Right: Rudyard's legendary burger.

Bottom Right: Football is best with friends and booze. Two handfuls of booze, preferably.

called Grown-Up Storytime, featuring original stories read by local comedians, actors, and performers.

Besides live music and events, there are pool tables, a shuffleboard table, and competitive, weekly dart tournaments. Rudyard's has much to offer, but the comfort, friendly service, and welcoming atmosphere are what cement this pub's status as a Houston institution. Also, an innovative food menu with monthly specials by Chef Jordan Economy adds new shine to the old favorites.

Leila Rodgers has been Rudyard's owner since purchasing the space in 1993. Traditionally bohemian and artsy, Montrose is a longtime hub for the LGBTQA+ community, but urban development, gentrification, and rising housing costs have changed the surrounding area.

No matter the changes in Montrose, Rudyard's remains part of what makes the neighborhood special.

2010 Waugh Drive, Houston
503-270-9258

There are so many amazing Vietnamese restaurants in Houston; it would be unfair to try ranking them all. Houston has the second largest Vietnamese community of any U.S. city, so authentic, delicious Vietnamese food can be found all over the place. Most everybody has a favorite place for pho or banh mi, and just about every neighborhood has a good Vietnamese place nearby.

Not every place does Cajun-inspired seafood boils, though, particularly not when Viet-Cajun fusion places in town have become media darlings from exposure on network television and celebrity chef travel shows. Using a blend of Vietnamese and Cajun flavors, ingredients, and techniques produces spicy crawfish in garlic butter sauce, Asian-inspired, but with traditional elements like potatoes, corn, and sausage chunks thrown into the seasoned boil.

Saigon House stands apart even in an already-crowded landscape of both traditional and Viet-Cajun fusion restaurants. The menu offers innovative dishes featuring snow crab, massive shrimp, and even lobster. Guests can select from a variety of inventive sauces and spice levels. And I don't know any other place that puts egg rolls inside of spring rolls. The house spring rolls feature the usual crunchy veggies and cold vermicelli. Then, a full pork and shrimp egg roll gets stuffed into the cylindrical rice paper wrapping.

Sizzling platters of perfectly seasoned shaken beef are analogous to a Vietnamese version of fajitas. Crisp peppers and onions provide crunch and flavor to the tender chunks of marinated steak, smoking and popping on cast-iron plates.

3103 Main Street
Houston, TX, 77002
713-529-1100, saigonhousefood.com

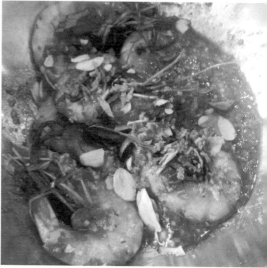

Top Left: House special roll, with an egg roll inside a spring roll.

Top Right: Shaken sizzling beef with added broccoli.

Bottom Left: Two of the seasoning options and the spice levels. Are you a dragon or a unicorn?

Bottom Right: Thai surprise shrimp, Angry Dragon spice level. Amazingly good.

ZEN IZAKAYA

Japan is possessed of fascinating language and complex culture. One of the more important cultural concepts that exists is that of Wa (和). In English, we would translate this as 'harmony,' but it is significantly more nuanced than that. Western culture would define it more as consequential ethics, such as the social contract theory.

Utilitarianism furthered this concept. It states that any course of action should promote happiness. Basically, "morality" implies the greatest amount of happiness among the greatest number of individuals in society should be the underlying directive in our conduct.

Western culture has never fully absorbed this in practice. We are too fiercely individualistic and self-centered. Not so in Japan. Even in densely populated cities like Tokyo there is zero litter, despite not having trash cans placed on every corner like in the States. People don't litter there. They wouldn't.

Tourists might, but someone would pick it up eventually, and not necessarily because it's their job. It's Wa, the proper, correct thing to do.

For the greater good.

At Zen Izakaya, this balance is well represented. Steady crowds speak for its quality, and the fact that most customers are speaking Japanese speaks for the authenticity. Zen Izakaya competes with a handful of remarkable Japanese restaurants in Houston, like Uchi and Kata Robata.

Both pay incredible homage to the source material and the kitchen staffs execute their concepts flawlessly; they are incredibly talented and well trained. At Zen, though, it is entirely different. It's a place where salary men legitimately gather to commiserate over beer and karaage.

One wouldn't think a mom and pop sushi joint in a strip mall would be so excellent, but Zen Izakaya would be the exception, not the rule.

Left: A lunch bento, which includes soup and a small salad.

Top Right: A fine selection of nigiri, all well cured, seasoned, and served at the correct temperature.

Bottom Right: Delicate garnish helps enhance the superb fish.

The quality of sushi is exceptional. Daily fish specials are flown in from Tsukiji, Tokyo's bustling epicenter of all things seafood.

Lunch is a great deal. Sizeable bento boxes are artfully assembled, bearing a mix of sides like pickled vegetables, salads, and makimono alongside mains like ebi tempura and teriyaki. A late afternoon happy hour can be pleasantly extended into early evening, and there is never a rush.

Explore the sake selections. Fans of the rice liquor can definitely find something good—dry, crisp, fruity, and even cloudy, unfiltered varietals. Classic Japanese soups like udon and ramen do just the trick on chilly winter evenings, however proportionally few such weather occurrences are in Houston.

2015 South Shepherd Drive, #700
Houston, TX 77019
346-800-1887, zenjapaneseizakaya.com

Fun fact: whenever sushi is served super cold, it likely means flavor is masked by the temperature. Sushi described as "fresh" just means the restaurant hasn't cured or properly aged certain cuts, which ensures enhanced flavor.

YO-YO'S HOT DOGS

Houston's highest-rated restaurant on Yelp isn't a steakhouse. The top restaurant in town, at least according to the people who take time to do things like rank restaurants on the Internet, isn't fancy or expensive. It's not some high-concept fusion or form of haute cuisine. There are no omakase, daily specials, or wine lists because it's not really a restaurant, and there really isn't even a menu.

It's a one-man food cart. That man is Yoyo—real name Daniel Kim—and all he serves are addictively delicious hot dogs.

Nathan's Famous hot dogs, topped with "All the Wrong Ingredients," according to their online menu. Each all-beef frank gets topped with cream cheese, curry ketchup, caramelized onions, fried onions, sriracha chili sauce, and honey mayo.

It sounds odd—and it is odd, at first—but somehow it all works. The onions are salty, sweet, crispy, and soft, all at the same time. Smeared on first, the cream cheese acts as a binder, both keeping the dog in place and the bun from getting soggy. It's decadent, particularly the honey mayo, which balances the kicked-up curry ketchup and mild sriracha bite.

Kim, who spent time working in the restaurant industry before

A Yoyo's food truck south of Houston has permanent location and hours. On Sundays the truck posts up at Fox Hollow, a bar off Washington. However, from Thursday through Saturday from 8:30 p.m. until 3 a.m., Yoyo's original stand is still operating. Lines can start forming before they start, but once up and running, Kim's wife helps him prep four dozen dogs at once with clockwork efficiency. Yoyo's dogs are quite possibly the perfect post-bar food, but don't let anyone take pictures while you're eating. It's… messy work.

YoYo's New York Style Street Dogs
$4

...an's Famous 100% All Beef Hotdog on a Toaste...

Fully Loaded aka "All The Way" ($4) for the BEST tast...

Cream Cheese
Spicy Mustard
Curry Ketchup
Grilled Onions

✓ Crunchy Fr...
Onions
✓ Honey Ma...
✓ Sriracha

Left: A whole mess of onions caramelizing to sweet, mushy-brown perfection on the flattop.

Middle: Fully dressed hot dogs.

Right: Yo-Yo's condiment menu, though it is strongly suggested to go "all the way." That's a lot of pressure, though, and no one should be pressured to go all the way if they aren't ready.

opening the tiny food cart in 2014, developed the recipe himself, wanting to create hot dogs distinctly reflective of Houston. Similar to the Chicago dog, served with very specific toppings, Kim aims to have his Yoyo dog become famous, known as the wiener towering above all others in Space City.

5555 Morningside Drive
Houston, TX 77005
713-839-6207, yoyoshotdoghtx.com

Mom and Pop restaurants are a dying breed. Continuous competition for market space amidst chains, well-funded restaurant groups, and fickle dining trends produces a harsh climate that can prevent independents from thriving.

Nonetheless, places like Sushi Miyagi succeed because of tireless commitment, consistency, and true dedication to customers. Originally from Okinawa, Chef Miyagi is a sushi chef with well over thirty years of experience. Miyagi-sama runs this humble Chinatown sushi bar with only his wife for help.

Visiting during peak hours requires patience, but Mr. and Mrs. Miyagi work diligently to accommodate their guests. Even during down times, as fast as they both move, things do not happen quickly, but it's worth the wait.

Chef Miyagi is a blur, personally preparing every sushi order with deft precision. His wife runs the back and front of the house, busses tables, and takes orders. There are times when both Miyagis seem to sprint around the place, running plates and filling sake cups. They are only open four days a week during limited hours—presumably to rest, but also to prepare, age, and plan each prime cut of fish.

First-time visitors to Sushi Miyagi need to look carefully for their small storefront. It's in a drab shopping center location, and the sign outside merely says "SUSHI," which can be a bit hard to locate.

Be prepared to wait during peak hours—it is quite literally a mom-and-pop place, and they are the sole employees. Patience is rewarded, however, in some of the finest Japanese fare Houston has to offer.

Top Left: Sake. Duh.

Top Right: Tuna and cucumber maki; "green monster" maki, with sinus-draining amounts of wasabi tobiko, crunchy, briny orbs of flying fish roe mixed with wasabi.

Bottom Left: Understated signage; or exactly stated signage. Go see for yourself

Bottom Right: Lunch menu. Great deals on handmade, high-quality and authentic Japanese food.

The sushi is art, comparable to anywhere else in Houston, and all at a pleasantly attractive price point. Fans of Westernized, mayo-heavy rolls will have ample options, but true aficionados of traditional, hand-formed nigiri and sashimi will find adherence to Edo-style austerity at Sushi Miyagi. There are great lunch specials like chirashi, a chef selection of sashimi over sushi rice or immaculately smoked unagi.

10600 Bellaire Boulevard
Houston, TX 77072
281-933-9112

THEODORE REX

Justin Yu definitely understands Houston.

While the Gulf Coast region is casually underappreciated elsewhere, Yu's travels, awards, and experience cooking at top restaurants around the country have perhaps provided some context for how special his home is.

At Oxheart, his 2012 debut, Chef Yu aspired to do incredible things—and it worked.

Oxheart won all kinds of awards, including a James Beard. Yu was named Best Chef Southwest in 2016, one of only three Houston chefs ever honored. For five years, Yu's team broke their backs reinventing everything about what a restaurant could be. They developed perambulating tasting menus, primarily focused on vegetables. Careful preparation techniques for each course required countless hours of combined planning and labor.

Such levels of focus and dedication made Oxheart one of the city's most famous restaurants and Justin Yu one of its best-known chefs. Then, in 2017, it closed. Weathering personal and professional growth, Yu took his restaurant in a new direction, or, rather, into a different plane of existence.

Theodore Rex emerged from the bones of Oxheart. It is something else, a new species evolved out of the million-and-one little varied expressions served over five renowned years. Yu's food is complex but never convoluted. It's high-concept and always refreshingly new and vibrant. But dining at Theodore Rex is relaxed and stress-free. It's a true experience; a bit of fun and excitement that can be found for the mere price of a meal.

It's special, an unexpected joy, and absolute culinary marvel.

1302 Nance Street, Unit A
Houston, TX 77002
832-830-8592, trexhouston.com

Top Left: Crispy rice and beans, swimming in butter and herbs.

Middle Left: Cantaloupe in herbs and a chilled broth.

Right: Located East of Downtown in an old office, the space is intimate, charming, and beautifully decorated.

Bottom Left: Wagyu, topped with an anchovy condiment and charred herbs.

191

My mom is really into bread. Like, way too into bread. So into bread that she has spent months googling "bread schools," "bread classes," and "how to learn to make bread." She hasn't had much success, but it's more likely a result of her being kind of bad at using the Internet rather than lacking the inherent skills required for baking.

Bread is now such an obsession with my mother it has become the focal point of nearly every conversation and interaction. It certainly comes up whenever dining out. Suffice it to say, wherever we go, the bread service better sparkle. Not surprisingly, I was apprehensive when she suggested we meet at Common Bond one morning. Common Bond is a bakery with pastries, breads, and desserts. Alcoholic drinks, coffee, and full menu service are available all day, as well.

We were supposed to meet at 10 a.m. My mom texted me at 7:30, letting me know she was there already. She was casing the place, basically, to check out the bread. Leaving a wet load of laundry to ferment, I hustled over to meet her.

"They don't make their bread here," my mom hissed when I arrived.

That was her complaint. Her only complaint, in fact. She found it disingenuous if not outright deceitful.

The real reason, I suspect, is that Common Bond has been so insanely popular since opening, they simply had no choice but to outsource some of their product. People love Common Bond's bread.

People also love their macarons, cookies, and custom cakes. If the serpentine weekend lines are any indication, people love their brunch, too. Even Plain Croissants are anything but, featuring 33 flaky layers of dough folded with cold butter, good as any Parisian pâtisserie.

Common Bond originally opened in 2014 by Houston native

Top Left: Latte art.

Top Right: Ayyybadaabummbaddumdabadumda AYYYYYYY macaroons. Aiiiiight.

Bottom Left: Pistachio croissants, scones, and muffins.

Bottom Left: A lunch spread of butternut squash soup, crostini, and roasted broccoli.

and acclaimed baker Chef Roy Shvartzapel, who partnered with mother-son team Kathy and Brad Sanders. Shvartzapel, experienced at some of the world's very best bakeries, departed a year later amid little fanfare. The business was sold in 2016 to Johnny Carrabba, a successful local restaurateur, and business partner George Joseph.

Carrabba wisely on kept most of Shvartzapel's hand-picked talent, promoting from within to ensure continuity during transition. A customer from day one, Mr. Carrabba saw potential in the business, acquiring it with an eye to grow. Plans for a second location in the Heights give every indication the group will... rise to the occasion.

1706 Westheimer Road
Houston, TX 77006
713-529-3535, commonbondcafe.com

THREE BROTHERS BAKERY

May 8th, 1945, began poorly for Sigmund Jucker. At least it started poorly, the same as any other day had during the last four years of his life.

In in the Nazi concentration camp where he resided, Jucker's job was waking his fellow prisoners each morning. But May 8th, 1945, would be different. It would bring an end to near constant suffering and pain.

The Allied Forces were approaching: it was Liberation Day. Realizing that the S.S. guards had fled, Sigmund located wire cutters and liberated himself, falling to kiss the free ground. His two brothers and sister survived, as well.

May 8, 1949, was also noteworthy for the Jucker family. Exactly four years after escaping the horrors of internment, Sigmund Jucker and his two brothers opened a bakery on Holman Street in Houston, Texas.

They named the place according to their kinship and quantity: Three Brothers Bakery.

There were no dough mixers; they stirred ingredients just like they

Very few times have the bakeries been forced to close: Hurricane Ike closed them for nine months in 2008. Amazingly, they paid their employees the entire time. It was also the only time the bakery had to restart their "sour," the yeast starter for most breads. Unfortunately, the Jewish high holidays also occurred during the Ike shutdown, causing a challah bread shortage in the Jewish community that made the front page of the *Houston Chronicle*.

Left: Three Brothers, four bracelets.

Right: Hamentashen, a tri-fold-hat–shaped cookie filled with fruit preserves. These tasty little triangles are served on the holiday Purim.

used to while growing up in in Poland.

Learning old country bakery recipes as young children laid the foundation for future success. Hand-mixing dough for pastries and bread was old hat. Not much changed over the next thirteen years it took for the brothers to hire another employee. Up until that point, they did it all themselves, and all by hand.

Today, there are three locations. And mixers. After almost seventy years of producing family-made baked goods for their neighbors around Houston, Three Brothers Bakery hasn't changed much. They haven't really needed to.

4036 South Braeswood Boulevard
Houston, TX 77025
713-666-CAKE (2253), 3brothersbakery.com

YOKUSHI ROBATA

Irori, which are traditional Japanese hearths, are sunken, ash-filled fire pits lined with a hearty and fire-resistant wood. Historically, Japanese homes were made almost entirely of wood and paper. An ever-burning fire pit in the middle of such a potential tinderbox makes practically no sense, and seemingly defies fire safety altogether.

However, irori were long a household fixture, providing insight into how Japanese families adapted to the restrictive nature of living on volcanic islands with limited natural resources, varied topography, and oft-harsh climate and geology. Yearly, about 1,500 earthquakes occur in Japan, with minor tremors happening somewhere almost daily. Larger events can produce devastating tsunami capable of unparalleled destruction.

Irori provided a home's central meeting place. Clothes could be dried, pots of water heated for tea, and there was ambient warmth in winter, allowing everyone to gather, eat, and commune. Irori also helped draw moisture from the wooden framing most homes were built from, preserving their integrity and lifespan. Of course, they were also used to cook.

Modern robatayaki, translating to "fireside grilling," draw inspiration from antiquity by cooking with a type of charcoal originally developed for use in irori. Known as binchōtan, these cylindrical charcoal briquettes burn hot for ages but produce minimal smoke. Binchōtan provide even cooking temperatures and distinct, slightly smoky flavors that make robatayaki special.

Famously, chicken skewers called yakitori are excellent examples of Japanese charcoal cooking. Visit one if ever in Japan. Watching the grill master is an inspiring portrait of devotion to perfection, even if they only cook chicken meats on little sticks. There is obsession with perfection in Japan, ever sought but never attained. Rather, dedication is everything.

Top Left: Katsu—a deep fried, panko-breaded pork cutlet served with tangy sauce and Kewpie mayo on a bed of cabbage.

Top Right: An artist at work—plus a ton of sake.

Bottom Left: Grilled shrimp in its purest form; lightly seasoned and brushed with tare sauce, finished with sesame seeds and even more damn cabbage.

Bottom Right: Charcoal and smoke.

Perfection is certainty. Certainty is arrogance, which runs contrary to a culture of self-effacement.

Not surprisingly, this form of singular obsession with craft can be found at Yokushi Robata, located on Richmond Avenue in Houston in a strip mall with all manner of good places to eat. Yokushi manages to easily stand out among the crowd.

Order some draft beer or something from the dynamic sake menu. Cold sake is definitely best with the smoky grilled meat and veggies. Servers can suggest how best to order, but including a plate of tonkatsu is simply a good idea.

Start with veggies and sweet, delicate seafood. End with the heavier chicken and red meat options. Everything is delicious and perfectly seasoned, meaning no dipping sauces.

Natural flavor is enough.

3837 Richmond Avenue
Houston, TX 77027
832-933-6888, yokushirobata.com

SAMMY'S WILD GAME GRILL

Everyone should try a camel burger at some point in life. Or python chili-cheese fries. Particularly, we should eat more kangaroo, especially for Australians.

Kangaroo populations are out of control Down Under, where the big-footed marsupials outnumber Homo sapiens two-to-one. Australia's government has initiated ongoing campaigns urging citizens to throw some 'roo on the barbie instead of shrimp. Florida has adopted similar practices, as have some Caribbean islands, attempting to curb the ecological impact invasive species like lionfish have on endangered coral reefs.

This kind of eating is definitely within the realm of possibilities at Sammy's Wild Game Grill. Owner Samuel "Sammy" Ballarin had this concept very much in mind when he opened in 2011. With a vision of bringing unprocessed, wild game to the masses, Ballarin packaged the unfamiliar proteins in familiar ways, like burgers, hot dogs, and tacos. While much of the menu is farm raised, organic, and free-range, some of the meats are hunted wild, like the aforementioned camel and kangaroo, as well as water buffalo and iguana. Sammy's menu varies by seasonal availability, but regularly features ostrich, emu, yak, and wild boar. In fact, there is even a diet specifically focused on such organic, free range, non-domesticated foods. Basically, exclusively eating anything one can pick, forage, hunt, or grow—sans any cultivation or human influence—is called a "wildatarian" diet.

Like most diets, it's largely nonsense.

Most eating and lifestyle fads simply have too few empirical data establishing efficacy, but some shreds of propriety invariably can be found amongst the varying bombastic claims.

Top Left: A small selection of the many ice cream products offered by Blue Bell.

Top Right: As Rihanna would say, "Birthday cake cake cake cake cake."

Bottom Left: Moo-llennium Crunch, one of the more popular flavors.

Bottom Right: Coach is very happy about his fudge bar. Maybe too happy. What's he up to?

RESTAURANTS A-Z

Al Quick Stop, 26
2002 Waugh Drive

Anvil Bar and Refuge, 18
1424 Westheimer Road

Axelrad and Luigi's Pizza, 2
3700 Almeda Road

Bacco Wine & Spirits, 134
5010 Dincans Street

Barbecue Inn, 12
116 West Crosstimbers Street

Barnaby's Cafe, 74
604 Fairview Street

Bernie's Burger Bus, 126
5407 Bellaire Boulevard Suite A

Blue Bell Country Ice
Cream, 200
1101 South Blue Bell Road

Bombay Pizza Company, 20
914 South Main Street, #105

The Breakfast Klub, 52
3711 Travis Street

Bubba's Texas Burger
Shack, 84
5230 Westpark Drive

Cafe Brussels, 82
1718 Houston Avenue

Camerata, 118
1830 Westheimer Road

Cleburne Cafeteria, 24
3606 Bissonnet Street

Common Bond, 192
1706 Westheimer Road

Conservatory, 28
1010 Prairie Street

Corkscrew BBQ, 106
26608 Keith Street

Dolce Vita, 56
500 Westheimer Road

Dollar Hot Dog Night at
Minute Maid Park, 32
501 Crawford Street

Don Café & Sandwich, 66
9300 Bellaire Boulevard

Frank's Pizza and Backyard, 36
417 Travis Street

Frenchy's, 124
3919 Scott Street

Gelazzi, 120
3601 White Oak Drive

Goode Company Barbecue, 4
5109 Kirby Avenue

Goodnight Charlie's, 42
2531 Kuester Street

Govinda's Vegetarian
Cuisine, 48
Hare Krishna Temple and
Cultural Center
1320 West 34th Street

H Mart, 16
1302 Blalock Road
9896 Bellaire Boulevard

Hay Merchant, 34
1100 Westheimer Road

Helen in the Heights, 116
1111 Studewood, Suite B

Hickory Hollow, 62
8038 Fallbrook Drive

Himalaya, 64
6652 Southwest Freeway

HK Dim Sum, 156
9889 Bellaire Avenue, #110

The Hobbit Cafe, 150
2243 Richmond Avenue

House of Bowls, 162
6650 Corporate Drive

Houston Livestock Show
and Rodeo, 72
NRG Parkway

Hubcap Grill, 70
1111 Prairie Street

Hugo's, 38
1600 Westheimer Road

Hugs and Donuts, 50
1901 North Shepherd Drive

James Coney Island
(JCI Grill), 170
Multiple locations

Kata Robata, 68
3600 Kirby Drive, H

Kenny & Ziggy's, 8
2327 Post Oak Boulevard

Killen's Texas Barbecue, 110
3613 East Broadway Street

King's Bierhaus, 132
2004 T.C. Jester Boulevard

Korean Noodle House, 76
10016 Long Point Road

La Guadalupana, 178
2109 Dunlavy Street

Lankford Grocery, 22
88 Dennis Street

Les Givral's Sandwich &
Cafe, 178
2704 Milan Street

Little Matt's, 108
6203 Edloe Street

Local Foods, 58
Multiple locations

Lone Star Beer, 174
Anywhere beer is sold

Lopez, 144
11606 Wilcrest Drive

Maine-ly Sandwiches, 112
7620 Katy Fwy. #225

Mala Sichuan Bistro, 136
9348 Bellaire Boulevard

The Maple Leaf, 6
514 Elgin Street

Melange Crêperie, 138
711 Heights Boulevard, B

Nam Giao, 160
6938 Wilcrest Drive, Suite C

Oishii, 130
3764 Richmond Avenue

One/Fifth, 114
1658 Westheimer Avenue

Oporto Fooding and Wine
House, 164
125 West Gray, #500

The Original Ninfa's on
Navigation, 140
2704 Navigation Boulevard

Pappa Geno's, 158
Multiple locations

The Pass & Provisions, 148
807 Taft Street

The Pastry War, 154
310 Main Street

Paulie's, 80
1834 Westheimer Road

The Pit Room, 166
1201 Richmond Avenue

Platypus Brewing, 104
1902 Washington Avenue,
Suite E

The Rice Box, 172
300 West 20th Street

The Richmond Arms, 122
5920 Richmond Avenue

Riva's Italian Restaurant, 40
117 Missouri Street

Roost, 176
1972 Fairview Street

Rudyard's British Pub, 180
2010 Waugh Drive

Saigon House, 182
3103 Main Street

Saint Arnold Brewing
Company, 142
200 Lyons Avenue

Sammy's Wild Game Grill, 198
3715 Washington Avenue

Sarah Place, 54
9968 Bellaire Boulevard, #160

Star Pizza, 30
2111 Norfolk Street

Sushi Miyagi, 188
10600 Bellaire Boulevard

Tan Tan, 78
6816 Ranchester Drive

Tex Chick Puerto Rican, 46
712 ½ Fairview Street

Theodore Rex, 190
1302 Nance Street, Unit A

Three Brothers Bakery, 194
4036 South Braeswood
Boulevard

Tiger Den Noodle House, 60
9889 Bellaire Boulevard,
Suite D-230

Voodoo Queen Daiquiri
Dive, 14
322 Milby Street

Whataburger, 146
Multiple locations

Yokushi Robata, 196
3837 Richmond Avenue

Yo-Yo's Hot Dogs, 186
5555 Morningside Drive

Zen Izakaya, 184
2015 South Shepherd Drive,
#700

APPENDIX